A
MAN FOR
ALL
SPECIES

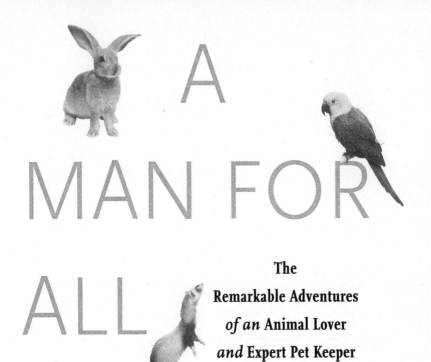

A MAN FOR

ALL

The
Remarkable Adventures
of an **Animal Lover**
and **Expert Pet Keeper**

SPECIES

MARC MORRONE *and* NANCY ELLIS-BELL

Harmony Books   New York

AUTHOR'S NOTE

Some of the people included in my book prefer to maintain their privacy, so I have either made reference to them without using their names at all or changed their names and other identifying characteristics to ensure that they will not be recognized.

Copyright © 2010 by Marc Morrone and Nancy Ellis-Bell

All rights reserved.
Published in the United States by Harmony Books, an imprint of the Crown Publishing Group, a division of Random House, Inc., New York.
www.crownpublishing.com

Harmony Books is a registered trademark and the Harmony Books colophon is a trademark of Random House, Inc.

Library of Congress Cataloging-in-Publication Data
Morrone, Marc
A man for all species : the remarkable adventures of an animal lover and expert pet keeper / Marc Morrone and Nancy Ellis-Bell.
p. cm.
1. Morrone, Marc. 2. Pet owners—United States—Biography. 3. Pet shop owners—United States—Biography. 4. Pets—United States—Anecdotes. I. Ellis-Bell, Nancy.
II. Title.
SF411.45.M67A3 2010
636.088'7092—dc22
[B]
2009042703

ISBN 978-0-307-58965-1

Printed in the United States of America

Design by Diane Hobbing of Snap-Haus Graphics

1 3 5 7 9 10 8 6 4 2

First Edition

To my mentor and friend
Martha Stewart, without whom this
book would not have been possible

CONTENTS

FOREWORD

by Martha Stewart

I "met" Marc Morrone one night, late, on Channel One, a Long Island cable station. I was flipping through the offerings when I saw a bespectacled youngish man standing behind a table covered—and I mean really covered—with every kind of domesticated animal and bird, and rodent and amphibian. The quantity of animals was astonishing, but even more unbelievable to me was the fact that all the animals were walking or crawling around unfazed, or fluttering or swooping on branches or perches above the table, oblivious of cameras and lights and hubbub. There were no squabbles that first half hour while I stood, transfixed on the screen, watching this nerdy, charming guy talk a mile a minute about all his "friends" in front of him.

The next morning I called him from my television studio and begged him to bring his menagerie to my show. He was an instant hit, and his knowledge and commonsense suggestions to pet owners and pet lovers everywhere has proved to me that he is the real thing.

After scores of appearances on my show, Marc has increased his following nationally as well as internationally, and his suggestions to the myriad questions he is asked weekly have proven to be practical, useful, and just plain good.

His story, told here in charming narrative, encourages us all to be better pet keepers. I hope you enjoy it as much as I have.

A WORD FROM JIM FOWLER

Marc Morrone and I are either "blessed" or "cursed" with a special kind of genetic programming that enables us to not only work with animals of all kinds, but also to educate people about the animal world. We are driven to raise awareness about all species—large and small, wild and domestic, commonplace and unusual. No living creature is deemed insignificant or disposable, and we believe that the survival of humans is linked with the survival of animals. That is our shared mission, to help save not only animals but all of the natural world.

When I was in fourth grade, I became fascinated with birds of prey and the art of falconry, the "sport of kings" during the Middle Ages in Europe. Even my name, Fowler, refers to someone who trains falcons and other predatory, hunting birds. Our family crest was and still is a hooded hawk on a raised glove, along with a lure. Even as a ten-year-old boy, my destiny was clear. For Marc, it was Gerald Durrell's determination to collect and study as many animals as he could. For me, at first, it was the wings in the air and those captured on our family crest.

As an adult, I became a professional lecturer about and trainer of those birds of prey. There were not only birds in my house, but a zoo of opossums, bobcats, snakes, weasels, and a host of other species, along with the customary dog. When I went on tour, I traveled with eagles, falcons, a cheetah named Arthur, and two giant anteaters named Lawrence and Florence. To get even "wilder," I traveled to Africa, where I trapped lions for a small budget film and later lived off the land with Kalahari bushmen. *Sputnik* for them was like "marsupial" to most Americans at that time.

After that I conducted the first studies of the giant Harpy eagle in the Amazon, a leviathan that ate thirty-pound monkeys as an appetizer. My studies completed, I brought two of them back to the United States, where I showed them to thousands of Americans on television. From there, I spent nearly thirty years with Marlin Perkins on *Wild Kingdom*. On leave from the show in the late 1960s, I also conducted the first studies of the giant Andean condor in Peru.

What I have done in my travels and in the media, Marc does in his business and as an educator and media personality. Occasionally, I appeared with him on *The Martha Stewart Show*, and such a pair we were.

Today, if you listen to any of Marc's lectures or radio programs, what you hear is his affection for all creatures great and small, weird or commonplace. In his live or television appearances, he is pictured with a menagerie of animals and his scarlet macaw, Harry, perched on his shoulder. Frequently, the animals he features become living ambassadors for the natural world, with Marc helping to deliver their message of hope for sustenance and survival. Whatever the environment—television, radio, his pet store, or educational lectures—this is a man of unflagging enthusiasm for the world of animals. The hamster is no less engaging than the noble parrot. The ferret is seen as a charming companion, and the simple goldfish is not so simple after all. After watching Marc talk about rabbits in one of his appearances, I told him afterwards that only he could make a rabbit interesting.

Marc is a man on a mission. We humans are responsible for the care and maintenance of our planet, and Marc is a tireless educator to that end.

I hope you read *A Man for All Species* with relish and delight. It is also a treasure chest of information on how we can best live with animals of all kinds—wild, captive, and domesticated. He is indeed "a man for all species." Welcome to his world, and yours.

Jim Fowler
Mutual of Omaha's *Wild Kingdom*
Former Wildlife Correspondent, NBC *Today* show
Honorary Member and Former Honorary President, Explorer's Club
Author of *Jim Fowler's Wildest Places on Earth*

PREFACE

I was a very young child, around five years old, when I began to think about having my own zoo. Of course, I was too young to understand the big concept of a zoo, but I did know that I wanted to collect and study as many animals as I possibly could.

By the time I started school, I was already transforming my bedroom, and then the front porch, into a "starter zoo" with specimens I had collected from a vacant lot down the street from my house in the seaside town of Long Beach, New York. My parents were exceedingly patient with my collection of insects and earthworms.

When I was eight years old and my family moved to Cold Spring Harbor, I started my first animal business, creating little vivariums and terrariums for neighborhood children. In high school, I expanded my elementary business into a bird-selling business that introduced me to the importing world. I was eighteen years old when I started Parrots of the World, opening my first store in Rockville Centre, Long Island, in 1978.

For thirty-two years I have imported, exported, sold, and cared for more animals than most people could ever hope to see in a lifetime. For the past twenty years I have shared my knowledge about animals and my experiences with America on media venues from local cable television to *The Martha Stewart Show,* where I am known nationally as the "pet keeper."

My pet-keeper status has also led me to four question-and-answer books with BowTie Press, and to the book you are about to read.

The reason I wrote this book is simple. Like Gerald Durrell, the famous animal collector and author who was my first mentor, I am compelled to share my knowledge with others—for the good of humanity and for the good of the animals in our care. Like Alba Ballard, the "Great Mother" of parrots, I am mandated to help anyone who asks for my assistance with one of their animals. Like Konrad Lorenz, acknowledged animal expert and noted author, I want people to know that hamsters are no less valuable as a pet than are dogs. Like Roger Caras, well-known media and dog-world authority, I speak to the masses about their lives with animals. And like Martha Stewart, my dear friend and media mentor, I entertain in order to teach.

Being the pet keeper is not without disappointments, trials, and controversy. I see everything, good and not so good, as part of the life I have chosen and accept.

It's good to be the pet keeper.

PART I

A PET KEEPER IS BORN

CHAPTER 1

Tiny Bones, Big Dreams

Long Beach, New York, in the 1960s was paradise for a child like me. Even though our house was small and there was no back-yard, it was only a short walk to reach the empty lot at the end of the block, an empty lot that became my laboratory for the natural world.

The vacant lot was overgrown with ragweed, briars, and poison ivy. There were also stands of milkweed and every stem had the caterpillar of a monarch butterfly clinging to it. I'd carry several of the caterpillars home to watch the chrysalis develop. Whenever I could be, I was down in that lot, catching every kind of insect I could find. Grasshoppers were one of my favorites because of how their mandibles worked. My maternal grandfather, Arnold, was proud of my bug collecting, and also that I knew what "mandible" meant. I had been reading since I was four, mostly *The Audubon Nature Encyclopedia,* and I always wanted to use the right word. My mother had bought me the books when she recognized my passion for bugs and other animals. My father was very quiet most of the time, but I knew he understood how important all creatures were in my life. But the most directly involved and expressive was definitely my grandfather.

"It's not big enough, Marc, not big enough."

He looked at the grasshopper I had caught and encouraged me to find an even bigger one. Some of the grasshoppers I caught were actually locusts and could fly, so I had a butterfly net to help. Off I went again in search of an even bigger bug.

On this occasion, I hit the jumping jackpot. I had walked behind the house, where I found the biggest grasshopper I had ever seen. It was enormous, at least three inches long, and it didn't have any wings. I crept up to it and grabbed it. Grandpa would be really proud of this one.

"Grandpa, look what I found!"

I could tell by the way he looked at my prize that it was indeed an excellent specimen.

"That's a big one, Marc. I can use that one to make my drawings."

My grandfather created the models for the Welch Biological Supply Company, and he worked from models based on real-life specimens. The grasshopper I had caught would enable him to capture the tiny details when he made his resin model. I was very proud of my contribution to his work.

There were some bugs I was never able to catch for him. He wanted a praying mantis, and I looked hard to find one. When I finally did find a mantis sitting on a branch, I was so mesmerized by it I couldn't move. The mantis turned its head toward me and just stared at me while it cleaned its front legs like a cat. It was like watching an alien life force. I was so fascinated by the way it looked that I didn't try to catch it. Another bug Grandpa wanted was a dragonfly, but I was terrified of those. They, too, were fascinating to watch, but someone had told me that they were like darning needles; if you grabbed one it would bite. It took me years to learn that this was false.

That may have been an old wives' tale; but the puffer-fish bite was a reality.

More than almost anything else, my grandfather loved fishing, and I was his constant companion on those outings. He kept his bait in the refrigerator drawer, usually live eels. Other times we'd dig with our pitchforks in the sand to find the best worms. Fishing with my grandfather wasn't just about fishing; it was about his sharing his knowledge of all living things. He knew how things worked, how legs worked, how mouths worked, and why they worked the way they did. He was a walking encyclopedia. Hanging out with him, I saw everything in living detail. I saw "how" worms and sand crabs buried themselves in the sand. I saw "how" birds dove underwater to catch fish. If I couldn't see "how" crabs were able to scuttle from side to side, my grandfather would explain it to me. If the crab was a female, and she was carrying eggs underneath her body, he explained why we had to let her go so that we would have more crabs the following year. I was always learning, learning, learning.

Except for the puffer fish.

We caught it by accident, and my grandfather put it in a bucket by itself.

"Don't touch it, Marc. Those fish have sharp, sharp teeth because of the crabs and shrimps they eat."

I looked at the fish and thought how remarkable it looked. Maybe just a little poke.

I screamed. The bite really hurt, not only because of the sharp teeth, but also because of my grandfather's sharp words. He explained again how those teeth worked. I truly felt like a hapless shrimp.

Our fishing expeditions were full of explanations and demonstrations. He "showed" me how a sea robin used its unusual fins by capturing one of the fish and putting it in one of his buckets. He "showed" me how the stinger works on a stingray we caught. He "showed" me how the flounder's two eyes move from the side of its head up to the top. When I was with my grandfather, I lived in a world of magic made real.

Away from the ocean and back in my neighborhood, my favorite captures were crickets, most of which I found in empty beer bottles and soda cans. I watched endlessly to understand more about them. I even fed them Cheerios so that I could observe how their mouths worked when they ate. The cricket has four jaws: one going to the right, one going to the left, one going up, and one going down. Like a little scientist, I studied how all four parts of the mouth moved up and down on the Cheerio. It was so rhythmic and precise. I also studied how their wings moved in order to make noise. If I had any questions, I went to the encyclopedia my mother had bought for me. Those books also taught me that when the female cricket breeds, she sticks her ovipositor directly into the soil. The crickets I caught lived in little jars in my bedroom, so they were always close at hand for observation.

Most children wake up in the morning to a room filled with toys and trinkets. I woke up to hundreds of eyes and thousands of legs.

For that reason, my mother rarely visited my room; and she didn't mind at all that I usually kept my door closed. I think she must have secretly worried that one of my specimens might escape somewhere into the house. Like the garter snake I had caught that did manage to find its way under the sofa. She still talks about that snake. I guess it made more of an impression than I thought.

"Hey, Mom, look at this one!"

I held up a small jar whose occupant was my prize catch so far.

"It's a special kind of cricket, and it spits out this nasty, black liquid when I pick it up."

My mother smiled. She really was proud of my scientific leanings. I decided not to share the fact that her little scientist had also tasted the black bile, and he knew it was bitter.

On Saturdays, my paternal grandfather, Pietro, would visit. Sometimes he would take me to the Bronx Zoo, where my favorite animals were the gorillas. At that time, they had a rare mountain gorilla, and at some point the gorilla disappeared. She probably died, but no one would tell the public what had happened. There are no mountain gorillas left in zoos today, only lowland gorillas, and I have tried unsuccessfully over the years to find out what her fate was. What I do know is that my zoo visits allowed me to get right up against the cages, and to not only see but also smell the animals. Children today can't usually do that, and I'm grateful that I was able to do so.

Grandpa Pietro truly understood me. He said that I had the "Morrone gene," a special gene that gave certain Morrone men the drive to understand and experience animals. He told me the story of his father, in Italy, who had rescued a lizard while out walking with some of his friends. His father had noticed a lizard just lying there in front of him on the path, and stooped down to pick it up. The lizard had become too cold to move, and so his father had picked it up and put it under his cap to get it warm again.

Most men would have simply stepped on or over the lizard, but not his father. When the lizard had regained its body heat, his father turned it loose farther down the path.

My grandfather went on to explain that it was probably someone with our kind of gene who first looked at a wolf and said to himself, "Maybe there's a way to make that wolf hunt for me." Or someone else like us who looked at a hawk that had just caught a rabbit, and thought, "Maybe I could hunt with that bird." That gene was definitely in our family, in me, but my father didn't have it at all. He did everything in his power to help me with my animal obsession, but he didn't share that gene with me and my grandfather.

It wasn't long before my bug collection expanded into creatures with bones, toads and frogs in particular. Now my bedroom was home to both chirping and croaking sounds. I also had goldfish and turtles that my parents bought me, but those pets didn't seem to last very long.

My first bird was a baby sparrow that I had found in the area behind our house. I took him home and fed him bread crumbs, because that's what everybody said you should feed birds. Only by chance, a neighbor named John Lombardi knew that you couldn't feed them bread, and he bought me a jar of mockingbird food that was in powder form. I mixed it with water; and sure enough, my sparrow survived. I raised him up, and mostly kept him in his cage. One day, he escaped from his cage and flew away. I was heartbroken. A few hours later, I went outside to play with some of my friends. Suddenly, one of my friends pointed up into the air behind me. He had this really astonished look on his face. I didn't see anything.

"What are you looking at?"

Whoosh! Something landed on my shoulder, and there he was. My little sparrow. I picked him up on my finger and took him inside to give him some food. For the rest of the summer, he flew loose in the neighborhood during the day. Then he would come home at night to sleep in his cage. I felt a little like Saint Francis.

For the rest of the summer, my feathered friend lived a perfect life—free by day, safe by night. One day, I returned from school and he wasn't there. I asked my mother what had happened, and she told me that she had seen him fly away with a little girl sparrow. I thought to myself, "How nice. He's going to live a happy life with another bird." It was five years later that my mother finally told me the truth, that my sparrow had been run over by a car. I would have preferred the happy life ending.

After the disappearance of my sparrow, I asked my mother if I could have a parakeet. My grandmother had parakeets, and I always thought it was funny how they would fly all over the house, and how some of them would land on my grandfather's beer glass and drink. I didn't quite understand why those birds didn't live very long. I still have the picture of me sitting in my grandmother's living room with a parakeet on my shoulder. I gave that picture to Martha Stewart, and it's one of her favorite pictures of me.

My mother said I could have my own parakeet, but I would have to save the money to buy one. I got a can, drew a picture of a yellow parakeet, and wrapped the picture around the can. Then I started collecting bottles and doing odd jobs, putting all my quarters into the can. Finally, I had enough to buy a parakeet, and my father took me to the pet department of a big department store. I remember that the canaries cost a whopping twenty dollars each, but the parakeets were only two dollars. I chose a yellow parakeet that I named Jinxie. I was absolutely fascinated by that bird. I'd watch it eat, I'd watch it preen. Everything it did was interesting to me. In order to hand-feed him, I dipped my finger in water and rolled it in the seeds. It was nearly magical to watch him use his little tongue to gather the seeds from my finger. Sadly, like most parakeets at that time, he didn't live very long. He probably died of a bacterial infection, caused by the water dish that hadn't been cleaned often enough. That's why today in my pet store, I insist that my employees wash every water dish with soap and water, every morning.

When my family decided to move to Cold Spring Harbor just before I started second grade, my passion for animals continued to flourish.

When I turned seven, I had already learned as much as I could about the natural world that Long Beach could offer. A new world was about to unfold—my parents decided to move to a new house in a more undeveloped part of Long Island.

CHAPTER 2

Big Bones, Small Business

Our new home was in Cold Spring Harbor, Long Island, where we had not only a bigger house but also a backyard. Now I had room to expand my collection to include salamanders, frogs, and birds. And there was a pond just three blocks away from our house, and woods that went so far past the pond that I couldn't see where they ended. I had found paradise.

It hadn't been easy moving my large bug collection to the new house, but both my parents and grandfather had helped me carefully load them up in the back of the station wagon. My new bedroom was even bigger, and we had an eight-by-ten-foot front porch. Mom agreed that I could use the porch for my "bones" collection, so now there was room for everything I wanted.

Truthfully, there was never enough room. One time, I found an enormous batch of frogspawn down at the pond, and I put it in a tub in the basement. To my great surprise, there weren't just frogs in that spawn. There were also salamanders and fish eggs mixed in with the frogspawn. When everything hatched out, I had my own little pond right there in the house.

I also had something that no other child in my school had: *The Audubon Nature Encyclopedia* in twelve volumes. My mother wanted me to be able to learn as much as I could about animals, not only from firsthand experience but also from books. I read every one of those books, some more than once. As a result, I became a very fast reader, an additional benefit to my animal education.

My biggest source for specimens was Titus Pond. The pond is still there, although less than half its original size and with very few species in residence. Approximately fifty by fifty feet at that time, the pond was home to more animals than I had ever seen in one place. Water bugs, frogs, tadpoles, painted turtles, carp, and the tiny, tiny spring peeper frog, all living in harmony among the cattails and water marigolds. Today, the pond is choked with weeds and hosts very little wildlife. But not then.

"Mom, I need some kind of net to catch things in the water." Both Mom and Dad were completely supportive of my animal habits and helped me in every way they could.

Mom immediately set about sewing a special net out of an old curtain, with a handle not too long, and the net surface not too big. It was perfect, and I set off like Huck Finn toward the great Mississippi.

In less than a month, the porch was filled with croaking frogs, chirping birds, and tongue-flicking snakes. Sparrows were my favorite, and they didn't seem to mind at all living in their small cages. With plenty of food and nothing to threaten their lives, they sang all the time. My mother liked them best of all, and she helped me to collect small twigs and such for their nests. Spring through winter, my menagerie lived outside no matter what the weather. No one seemed to mind, including the sparrows that continued to sing in the snow.

With the front porch at full capacity, I began to think of ways to save money for the animals I wanted to purchase someday. Given how easy it was for me to collect toads and frogs in particular, I decided to go into the terrarium business. While others had lemonade stands, I offered amphibians.

It started one summer when friends and I decided to do something different. Instead of selling lemonade like the other kids were doing, we went to the pond and caught tadpoles, frogs, baby toads, and even carp. We brought them back to my house and made terrariums and mini-aquariums out of Mason jars and whatever else we could find. We built a stand across the street and I sold everything we had caught. At age eight I had started my first "pet store" stand. I was beginning to realize that owning a zoo might be out of the question, but at least I would be able to have a pet store. I was also learning about so many species because different animals were coming and going all the time.

It wasn't only animals I was learning about. My mother loved gardening, and so I learned a lot about plants as well. That knowledge would come in handy later on when a nursery went into business across the street from our home.

That first year in Cold Spring Harbor also saw the arrival of my first cat, Kitty. A jet-black stray, Kitty adopted me, and my parents agreed to let him stay. For five years, until I was twelve, he was my "collection partner," bringing me specimens that I would never have been able to catch on my own.

He brought me shrews, chipmunks, and quail and other assorted birds. Whenever I could, I rescued these animals from the jaws of death and added them to my collection. The prize of his pursuits was a star-nosed mole that he brought back to me alive and no worse for the capture. I was fascinated by the way the mole's nose worked, along with his specially designed digging claws; he lived there on the front porch along with the rest of my "family." Most people never get to see a shrew, but Kitty especially liked to catch those. I was amazed to discover that one shrew ate one hundred fifty earthworms in one day. I knew that for a fact because I fed the shrew the worms and kept count. Once I'd studied a shrew, I would turn it loose. There was only so much room.

I was ten years old when I met Russell Taylor and my life changed forever. He and his family lived on a fifty-acre, nonworking farm not too far from where we lived. They reminded me a little of the Beverly Hillbillies, living there in the middle of the forest with their chickens, cows, ducks, and every kind of animal I wanted. They were also avid naturalists and birders, and I learned so much from Russell's father, who watched birds professionally and even counted them for field guides and other publications. Every Christmas, I would join Russell and his father for the annual bird count. I was also able to study bird banding with Russell's father, who was a master bander. I was very impressed, because even today there are very few master banders in the United States. I realized how fortunate I was to be surrounded by people—my family and the Taylors—who provided me with the perfect childhood for my animal dreams.

Even my teachers seemed to understand my young passion. One in particular, Mrs. Dorn, didn't find it strange when my little flock followed me to school. By the fifth grade, I had a black and white Birmingham roller pigeon named Lockey and a North American crow named Poe. It wasn't uncommon to see them flying behind me as I left home. The pigeon usually got lost, but Poe arrived when I did. Most of the time, he stayed outside; but on this one occasion, he flew into the classroom through an open window. He flew all over the classroom, probably looking for me. I was hiding my head inside my desk. It was one thing for him to follow me *to* school; it was quite another to have him joining me *in* school. The other kids were laughing, and I thought for sure they were laughing at me. I was also afraid that I would get in trouble for having a crow in the classroom. Mrs. Dorn was very calm about the whole thing.

"Oh, class, look at that crow."

Poe did not see me in the back of the classroom and was staring intently at Mrs. Dorn.

"Class, does anyone have some leftover lunch to share with the bird?"

One of the girls in my class pulled out a half-eaten sandwich and offered it to Poe. Poe grabbed the sandwich and flew back out the open window. He reminded me of Peter Pan. Sadly, Poe's life was not as magical as Peter Pan's. The next day, Poe drowned in our backyard fish pond. That memory of him in our classroom is a very special one.

Another profound loss was that of my much-loved cat, Kitty, who disappeared just after my twelfth birthday. Easter Sunday that year was not about bunnies and painted eggs. Kitty was gone and no one in my human family seemed to know what had happened to him. For days and weeks, I cried harder than I had ever cried for anything or anyone. Kitty wasn't just a great hunter; he was a creature who understood my passion and who devoted every day of his life to helping me build my dream. Cats have been close to my heart ever since.

My most unusual cat while growing up was Frosty, another stray who wandered into our backyard when I was fourteen. A huge tabby, he was smelly and dirty, and he never tried to come into the house. Instead, he loved to take long walks with my dogs and me, sometimes as many as five miles at a stretch. People would stare at the gangly adolescent with the long hair and glasses being followed by at least one dog and a determined cat. Frosty, too, went the way of Kitty and disappeared suddenly from my life a couple of years later.

It wasn't until years later that my parents explained why both cats had been so mysteriously dispatched. Kitty was whisked away because they feared she would suck the breath out of my newborn sister, a common superstition among not only Italians but many Americans as well. Frosty "disappeared" because he was so dirty and smelly. Today, I understand my parents' rationale, but as a child I only understood terrible, unexplained loss. Even today, I still think of Kitty and miss his feline simpatico quality.

Missing cats aside, my parents loved me dearly and would do anything for me, their beloved firstborn son. When our sixth-grade class, under the helpful guidance of Mrs. Dorn, decided to hold a carnival to raise money for the school, I came up with the idea of a carnival where students could throw Ping-Pong balls into tiny goldfish bowls and win a fish in a bowl. Mrs. Dorn gave me nine dollars to buy as many fish as I could, and keep them at my house until the day of the carnival. My parents drove me to the pet store where my nine dollars bought two hundred little goldfish that we put into a big plastic container. That night, when my father got up to check on the fish, he discovered that most of them were at the surface, gasping for air. Enlisting my mother's help, the two of them transferred goldfish into every available container they could find, including my father's prized Victorian teacup collection. In the morning, I awoke to a house filled with goldfish in every room and in every imaginable container. A house filled not only with tiny fish, but also with immeasurable love.

There are so many memories of my parents, my grandfather, the Taylor family, and others too numerous to mention who not only encouraged me, but also inspired me. There was the case of the skimmer birds that I correctly identified at the beach, while Grandpa Arnold insisted they were another species. When I showed him the picture in the encyclopedia, he insisted that the book was wrong. I was right, and he respected that I stood firm, even if it meant he was wrong. I remember the time the garter snake got loose in the house, causing my mother to approach every corner or hidden space with trepidation. She still talks about that snake, only now she laughs about it. There's the image of her making the fishing net for me so that I could catch specimens in Titus Pond. And there's that lovely image of my father using his prized teacup collection for needy goldfish.

When I look at my own son, I understand and accept that he doesn't have the same Morrone animal gene that I do. I just wish he could experience a small part of the joy I experienced as a child with the animals I collected and studied. He has his own kind of joy.

CHAPTER 3

A Store Is Born

High school was a challenging time for me. Some of those challenges eventually led me into my lifetime passion and career as the pet keeper, while others literally threw me to the ground. In high school, my friend Russell introduced me to my earliest mentor, Gerald Durrell. Here was a man who knew and understood animals, who had his own zoo, who wrote books, and who lived his life with and for animals.

My real life meant that most of the other kids teased me about my fascination with animals. It didn't help that I was skinny, had long hair, and wore glasses. The perfect target for bullies.

One particular group frequently harassed me on my way home from school and at the local hangout on Midland Street, about four blocks from my house. Mostly it was verbal taunts and name-calling, but on one occasion the attack was all-out physical. I had one ally. His name was Pancho.

Pancho was a Mexican Red-Headed Amazon parrot who frequently followed me to school, along with some of my pigeons and **other parrots**—as had my crow, Poe. It wasn't uncommon for my birds to fly loose in the neighborhood, and no one thought anything about it. It wasn't so much that Pancho was intentionally protective; like other parrots he was curious about where I was going and what I was doing. On this particular day, I was on my way to the hangout on Midland when I heard the approach of tires behind me on the sidewalk. Bike tires. Stingray bike tires, specifically, and riding those bikes hard were the bullies who most disliked me. They had beaten me up before, although never badly enough to send me to the hospital, and I had become stoic about the random attacks. Like the birds I had come to understand, I accepted random acts; that acceptance was part of their genetic makeup and mine.

Screech! The bikes came to a halt and three guys were on me like the proverbial stink on s—t. I curled into a fetal position to mitigate the blows, waiting for the barrage to be over. Then I heard a scream. It wasn't mine.

I looked up to see Pancho on the ground next to the boy's feet. Apparently, Pancho had decided to fly down from the trees and see what was going on. An Amazon parrot, like all parrots, will fluff up and spread its wings and tail when excited, so as to appear much bigger than it really is. Then, of course, there is the beak. For someone who doesn't know birds, and the bullies definitely didn't know birds, this sight must have been terrifying. Here was this agitated bird dashing madly around their feet. They had no way of knowing what kind of damage this bird could cause, and . . . it could fly. I watched from the ground as they scrambled toward their bikes, jumped on, and took off at warp speed. Pancho acted as if he didn't understand what all the fuss was about.

The bullies never bothered me again. Pancho became "the bird that saved my life," even if that was never his intention. Most likely he was just looking for something to eat.

It was also never my intention to transform my job at the local plant store into a bird business. I was fifteen and the store was right down the street from my house, so it was a convenient short walk. The two men who owned the store sold only indoor plants, especially bromeliads they imported from a special source in Holland, and they had a monopoly in the area. The bromeliads had tiny root systems and were grown hydroponically, giving them big, beautiful leaves and flowers. The owners would pot the little plants, and sell them wholesale to other flower shops and plant stores throughout the tristate area.

I had grown plants since I was a small child, so I felt confident that I could do a great job. I knew that because these plants had been grown hydroponically, their tiny root systems were not accustomed to dirt. This meant that the mixture I used had to be light and fluffy, with lots of peat moss and vermiculite. For those who don't know vermiculite, it is expanded mica that helps to "aerate" the soil mixture. I also knew that the roots and the crown of the plant had to be placed just right. The soil had to cover those roots, but not any of the leaf structure.

I had planted about a hundred of them when the main boss walked in.

"Oh, no; that's no good at all."

"What do you mean, it's no good?"

I wasn't being argumentative. I just didn't understand why he would say that.

"No, watch: when you pull on the plant, the whole thing comes out of the pot."

And with that, he grabbed a leaf and lifted the entire plant up out of the pot. He went over to where I'd mixed the soil—light and fluffy—and added a bunch of clay. This made my soil mixture relatively heavy. Then he took one of the bromeliads, dumped out the soil in the pot, filled it halfway with pure clay, and plunked the plant down into the clay halfway up its crown. As I watched, he packed the rest of the pot with the clay-soil mixture, and pounded it down with his fist.

"Now it's potted correctly."

This time, when he picked up the plant by its leaves, the entire pot came up in one piece.

"But the plants are going to die."

To me, this plant was a close relative to animals, and I was horrified.

"Don't worry. It's not gonna die here; it's gonna die somewhere else."

That was my first introduction to "real" business, and I decided right then and there that I would not do business that way.

That better way got its start right across the street from my house. I quit my job for the houseplant guys, and got one working for a red-haired Irishman named Bob Jack who had opened a small nursery where everything he grew was in the thousands. I'd pot a thousand roses, a thousand chrysanthemums, a thousand of whatever he was selling. I raised them from cuttings. I pinched them, fertilized them, grew them, nurtured them, and then I had the satisfaction of watching Bob sell them. I could have spent my entire life doing that except that my main fascination was with animals.

Bob also loved birds. At his home, he had aviaries where he kept pheasants, ducks, cockatiels, and Australian parakeets. Since we lived across the street from the nursery, my dogs and cats would follow me when I went to work. My birds would also follow me to his place, and they helped reduce the tedium of my planting and weeding tasks. There I'd be among the weeds, with my pigeons and Amazons overseeing my progress.

As my bird collection grew, Bob allowed me to put some of my "overflow" birds in an aviary on his property. For two years, until I opened my first store in 1978, my fledgling bird business kept its stock in my backyard and at Bob's nursery. Most of the birds I was selling were African Grey parrots, Amazons, cockatiels, conures, and Senegal parrots—birds I still sell today. I'm sure people might wonder how a sixteen-year-old kid knew how to import birds at such a young age; in those days, you could find whatever you wanted in Arthur Freud's *American Caged-Bird Magazine*. All I needed was money to buy what I wanted. I also gave Bob a cut of my profits, so he was a very happy guy.

When I finally left there to open my first store, I left behind a yellow-naped Amazon and a hybrid conure that seemed very much at home in their environment. Those birds are still there today.

Every year on Memorial Day, I go back to Cold Spring Harbor, because that's where both my grandfather and Alba Ballard (whom you'll meet in Chapter 5) are buried in the local cemetery. I carefully weed the graves and plant new flowers. Then I go to the nursery to visit my bird friends and walk around the old place. I never introduce myself to anyone. Bob is long since gone, and I know the birds don't recognize me anymore. Still, I say hello to them for old times' sake. The nursery now has a small petting zoo and a butterfly garden, but what I still see are the thousands of roses and chrysanthemums, and all those birds that launched me into business. I don't really believe in halcyon days, but I do acknowledge a certain kind of nostalgia for simpler days.

I wouldn't change a single feather.

CHAPTER 4

Harry and the Hyacinth Heist

As a child I had always been fascinated by birds of all kinds, from sparrows to finches to cockatiels. My front porch "zoo" in Cold Spring Harbor, Long Island, was home to many species, and thus began my long relationship with birds. Just before I turned thirteen I acquired my first "exotic bird," an African Grey parrot named Coco. By that time I had become curious about teaching birds to talk, so Coco became my first—and last—subject. It really wasn't hard at all, and it made me wonder what the big deal was about talking birds. I became more interested in the sounds birds make, and in learning to communicate with them through their natural sounds. Today I pride myself on understanding every sound a bird makes, including little naked baby birds whose noises to most people just sound like high-pitched squeaks. However, Coco's talking ability made him valuable, and I sold him for a great deal of money. I used that money to buy more birds to learn about.

After Coco, I began to develop my bird business in earnest. I had known from the time I was very young that I wasn't going to become a veterinarian or biologist. I wasn't an academic and didn't want to go to college. Even if I had been smart enough for college, I couldn't have afforded that kind of extensive education. So importing birds, and later other kinds of animals, would allow me to both study animals and, I hoped, make a good living. At the beginning, my total focus was on importing animals that I could sell, even before I had a store.

At the same time I started my bird business, I also became obsessed with the Masterpiece Theatre series *I, Claudius.* I quickly went from Long Island Italian boy to Roman parrot-ician.

In 1978 I imported two baby scarlet macaws from Guatemala; I named them Harry and Larry. Larry died while still in quarantine, but Harry survived and found his way into my life. I didn't have a store then, so my backyard was filled with cages, housing an assortment of small to large parrots.

Harry didn't like the idea of being someone's pet at all, so it turned out he was too nasty to sell. I did use him a lot in photography because he was certainly beautiful to look at—but not to touch.

Much kinder and sweeter were the hyacinth macaws, and I had great success with selling those. I imported them out of Paraguay, something you can no longer do because the number of hyacinth macaws worldwide is threatened. True to my obsession with *I, Claudius,* I gave all the birds Roman names, including the one I christened Remus. He was much smaller and shier than all of the others, so I decided to keep him.

Today, he is, I believe, one of the oldest, if not *the* oldest, hyacinth macaws in captivity. When I first got him, he lived in the backyard in a large chain-link cage with the other macaws, except for Harry, who at that time lived in the house with me. With the arrival of the hyacinths, I moved Harry outside with them where they all shared the same big cage. All four—Harry, Remus, Caesar, and Rosie—not only shared a cage, they shared the sky. I allowed them to fly free part of the time, just as I had with the sparrows and finches, all of which would come back to their cages. Only once did Harry and Caesar fly up into a cherry tree, which they refused to leave. Reluctantly, and to avoid any future mishaps, I had their wing feathers trimmed. Only once. Since that time, Harry's wings have never been clipped. This avian business venture gave me hope that I might be on a purposeful path to my own zoo, someday. My first pet store was a significant step toward that goal.

That goal was severely challenged on Groundhog Day of 1980. By that time, my partner and I had managed to open a small pet store of our own in Rockville Centre, New York. Compared to my backyard/bedroom-based business, that first store seemed huge and cost a whopping $700 a month in rent. In sharp and often terrifying contrast, my current store, Parrots of the World, which opened in 1999, is huge, with two floors, and costs me a staggering $16,000 a month. Success doesn't come cheap.

Back to Groundhog Day: I was busily dealing with hungry baby birds when three men walked in brandishing guns. The guys told me to put birds in boxes, pointing to which ones they wanted. I was twenty years old at the time, and I didn't consider myself especially brave. Besides, they had guns. So one bird at a time, I put into assorted boxes a hyacinth macaw, a scarlet macaw, a green-wing macaw, an African Grey, and many, many others. By now the initial fear had gone, and I was becoming decidedly angry.

It was at that point that one of the gunmen told me to put Harry in a box. I snapped.

"No, I won't do it. You have plenty of birds already. You can't have him."

The gunman looked surprised that some skinny kid was telling him, the guy with the gun, what to do.

"I said, put him in the box."

While the two of us faced off with each other, I noticed that Viking, the green-wing macaw, had climbed out of the box and had disappeared into the back room. The gunmen never even saw him, and his escape gave me additional courage.

"Go ahead," I said, "If you want to shoot me, shoot me, but I'm not going to give you that bird."

To my utter surprise and relief, the robbers left with what birds they had and I surveyed the damage. The value of the birds was in the thousands of dollars, and suddenly my courage gave way to near despair. The police who investigated the robbery did their best, but the robbers were never caught.

Harry looked at me in a gentle way—yes, a gentle way. I had sent him off to a breeder in Texas only a year or so earlier to see if I could create some "baby Harry's," but in the Lone Star State, Harry had been put in a cage with a big, nasty female macaw whom he immediately hated—and who he proceeded to kill, along with two birds in the adjoining aviary, into which he burrowed. Needless to say, he came back to me within weeks. Harry wasn't a bad bird around me, just around other parrots. Unlike most parrots, who will breed easily and without injuring their partners, Harry was unusually aggressive. After that I never tried to breed him again.

But in this moment, something had turned over in Harry, and a new bond had been created between us. To this day, some thirty years later, he is my constant companion, frequently appearing with me on *The Martha Stewart Show*. Martha knows better than to try to touch him. He's a one-person bird, no exceptions. Nor is he especially fond of other birds that seem to be getting my attention. Both Martha and I remember vividly the cockatoo caper.

Coral Ann, whom I still have and who is frequently seen on Martha's show, is a beautiful Moluccan cockatoo and is Martha's favorite among all my birds. Truth is, Martha adores that bird, and the problem with Harry on this one particular occasion may have started with that adulation.

In a famous scene, often replayed on Martha's Bloopers, Coral Ann sits on Martha's shoulder, and certainly the camera was giving all of its attention to the white bird. The red bird on my shoulder didn't like sharing the spotlight, and he grabbed for Coral Ann's feathers, ripping off her entire crest. Coral Ann screamed, Martha screamed, and there was Harry with a beak full of feathers. Now I screamed.

"Harry, what did you do?"

Silly question. I knew exactly what he had done. I pulled the feathers out of his mouth and gave him a withering look. Withering looks don't work very well with parrots. He looked most satisfied.

"Here," Martha said, "give them to me. I'm going to keep them in my dressing room."

To this day the feathers are still there, and no one competes with Harry for camera time. On camera, Harry's biggest interest was always my glasses. I have no idea how many pairs I've gone through. He loved pulling them off and chewing them; everybody thought it was cute. My optometrist loved it.

On one show, Harry went through six pairs of glasses. For a while, Martha's people tried to convince me that I should wear expensive, designer glasses. After Harry turned several pairs into pretzels, designer glasses became a thing of the past. Eventually, like all parrots, he got bored with bending eyewear; and today, the worst that he does is lick the lenses.

Away from the show and back in my pet store, Harry just hangs out in his cage, content to play with his toys and eat his food if I'm not there to play with him. When I have time, I let him out of his cage, plunk myself down in the middle of the floor, and sit there cross-legged. He walks over, and I tickle and scratch his head, which he absolutely loves. If I have time, he'll let me do that for half an hour or more. Other times, he'll lie on his back, and I'll rub his stomach or play bicycle with his feet. All the parrots I've ever known love to play on their backs. I've even seen people hold them upside down, and the bird seems to think it's a great game.

What so many people don't realize is that parrots live in the moment, and they're very good at entertaining themselves. If their human friend is there, fine; if not, they'll find another way to amuse themselves. Harry knows I am always there for him, whether or not he's in his cage. We're very old friends—the best kind of friends, as my grandfather would say.

CHAPTER 5

The Secret Life of "Flap-Flap"

In 1978, a human "best friend" came into my life. Everything I know about birds, especially parrots, I learned from Alba Ballard.

Alba was raised in Milan, Italy, where her family ran a zoo. She had come to the United States in her twenties, along with her husband and small son. I was eighteen when I met her in 1978. She lived around the corner from me; but all that time I was growing up, I had no idea I was living so close to a legend. Her greatest love was parrots and she had at least fifty of them. Godfather was a Triton cockatoo, and one of the rarest subspecies in that group. Both his face and crest were radically different from other Triton cockatoos, and to this day I've never seen another one like him. He was probably a subspecies from an island in Indonesia where cockatoos are widely diversified. Alba had acquired him in Europe and brought him to the United States, along with most of the other parrots she had. She also had other species of birds ranging from cranes all the way down to pigeons. She also had dogs, cats, and a wide assortment of other animals, including a kangaroo. Her garden looked as if it belonged in an Italian villa, with figs, oleanders, and fuchsias; it literally dripped with color and scent. Everything about Alba was exotic.

She also loved to cook, and she could fix a gourmet meal from the simplest of ingredients. Most of the time I visited, she would fix a meal for me, her husband, Marvin, and son, Claudio.

What usually took me to the table was an issue with a bird.

"Marc, I have bird with broken leg. You help me, I make you food."

Alba knew that I had a special way of restraining a bird so that it didn't get hurt while I treated a wounded wing or leg. I was happy to go over and help her with the little bird. It didn't take long, and then, poof, there on my plate was a fried egg mixed with potatoes and peppers, herbs and spices, and delicious!

And it wasn't just her family and me that she cooked for. She cooked food for all of her animals, designing special diets for each one. Alba taught me how to properly feed birds and keep them in optimal health. Back in the 1980s, the advertising agency for Friskies cat food asked her to do a commercial. By that time, Alba had become famous for her trained animals, including those she dressed up in costumes, and she was everybody's first choice for an animal promotion. The problem was she would have to fly to California, and she was afraid to fly.

"Alba, how many times will an opportunity like this come along?"

"No, I no fly."

That was it, and another masterful animal trainer whom I know well, Ray Berwick, was called in. He's the same one who trained all those birds in the movie *The Birdman of Alcatraz*. He also trained the crows in Alfred Hitchcock's movie *The Birds* and Lala, the cockatoo who appeared on *Baretta*. The birds he costumed for the ad looked wonderful, but not to Alba.

"Look, see how the costume is made like this? You know, I do better."

"Doesn't matter, Alba; you weren't there. They had to make the ad, and they couldn't get you to fly."

"Not good costumes."

Dressing up birds in costumes is probably what most people remember about her. She especially liked doing birthday parties for children, for which she would choose a particular set of caricatures or celebrities and outfit her birds accordingly. She also loved big events where her birds could add a whimsical element. For the 1976 bicentennial she staged a photograph called "The Spirit of 1776," for which she used an orange-winged Amazon named Tonto, a black-headed Caique named Bandito, and a mitred conure named Coo-Coo. There they were, three authentically costumed birds portraying the piper, the drummer, and the flag-bearer. That photograph helped make her even more famous.

Not that some people didn't complain about the inappropriateness or "cruelty" of what she was doing. What those people didn't realize was that the birds actually enjoyed getting dressed up. They were used to having their backs touched, so it was nothing for Alba to wrap a little costume with artificial arms around a bird's back and then secure it with a bit of Velcro. The birds could walk around unimpeded, and they loved the attention they got. Anyone who's ever been around parrots knows that they love exuberant praise and applause. These parrots were in their element.

Two of the parrots were in their element when Kathi and I got married. We had chosen the Westbury Manor for the ceremony and reception, but money was tight. What to do? As it turned out, the owners wanted birds to grace their gardens, so I traded them fancy ducks for the pond, a flock of peacocks for the grounds, and a Moluccan cockatoo in exchange for the cost of the wedding. Of course, I brought my own birds, including my Harris hawk, Stella; my scarlet macaw, Harry; and a flock of white homing pigeons that were released after we exchanged our vows. "Standing up" for us were two of Alba's parrots, both cockatoos, handsomely dressed as the bride and groom. One of our wedding photos shows the birds standing in front of Kathi and me, looking most pleased. They didn't need words to convey the sentiment of the occasion.

Alba always got the last word. Several years later, she was in the Woody Allen movie *Broadway Danny Rose*, in which she played a crazy woman with a ridiculous number of birds. She was also on *The Late Show with David Letterman* with her costumed birds. Both shows in New York, of course.

Then there was that *Gary Shandling Show* in which a heavyset woman with a Russian accent played another eccentric bird lady. It was obvious that the character was based on Alba, and at first Alba was upset by the caricature.

"Alba, you need to remember that imitation is the greatest form of flattery."

Even as I said the words, I also knew how hurtful it was for Alba to appear on so many television shows with her birds and be in some way ridiculed or made fun of by the hosts. The television personalities on whose shows she appeared were only interested in making the audience laugh, most of the time at Alba's expense. They weren't interested in truly educating their viewers, and that's still true today. When both my agent and editor talked to me about my doing television appearances, I wasn't at all excited, and I told them what I had told Alba after the *Gary Shandling* experience.

"The only reason those people bring you on their shows is to make fun of you. They make it sound as if they're going to share important information about this animal or that animal, but it's really all just about making people laugh."

Alba kept going on those shows even though she knew she would be a comedy catalyst. I suppose I will follow in her footsteps, if only to raise awareness for the animals I present or discuss.

As the producers of the *Shandling* show used to say when one of the guests canceled, "Let's bring on the bird lady."

Alba's performing career wasn't what endeared her to me. The most important thing about Alba was that she had learned everything she possibly could about all birds. Much of that knowledge came from her careful observations and insights. She had an instinct beyond that of anyone else I've ever met. In particular, Alba was an expert when it came to sick birds. Back in the 1970s, we didn't have the diagnostics that we have today. Sick birds were a mystery to most people, and most diagnoses and treatments were on a hit-or-miss basis. Alba had an uncanny way of knowing exactly what was wrong with the bird and how to treat it. She also knew instinctively whether the bird was going to die, no matter what treatment was tried. This was especially true of certain viruses. Sometimes, though, Alba was able to keep the infected bird alive long enough for its natural immune system to throw off the infection. She had special ways of feeding and regulating temperatures that seemed to produce miracles.

I clearly remember one time when I had a baby macaw that did not look as healthy as I thought it should. I couldn't tell if it was truly sick or just a healthy bird that was slow in growing.

"So, I've got this baby macaw and he's not growing very quickly. I don't know if he's sick, or if he doesn't like the food I'm giving him, or what's wrong."

Alba spoke as always in her special kind of broken English, her diagnostic questions somewhat cryptic as a result.

"Well, do he do 'flap-flap'?"

"Yes, he does 'flap-flap.'"

Translation, learned from spending so much time with her: When a baby bird is healthy, it's growing and will exercise its wings by grabbing hold of its perch or something on the floor and spreading its wings as far out as they will go. Then it flaps them as fast as it can while standing in place. If a bird can do "flap-flap," it's healthy.

"If he doing 'flap-flap,' he healthy. Don't matter what you see."

There it was. Simple but profound knowledge that has helped me immeasurably over the years. Alba was the consummate pet keeper. She could look at an animal and determine what was wrong just by the way it moved, the way it ate, the way its eyes worked. Like Gerald Durrell, she had that special spark, that "third eye" for the animal world.

She and I also shared a very special bird, a white-crested laughing thrush named Joker. He was the apple of my eye. He would fly out of his cage, land on my finger, and sing right into my face. He lived in my store, and one day—nearly thirty years ago—Alba came into my store to visit and to see what new birds I might have.

"Oh, that's a beautiful bird. You have to give it to me."

She wasn't kidding. Even though she didn't use those exact words, this was obviously a case of eminent domain. Alba knew that I knew that she had saved me thousands and thousands of dollars by helping me take care of birds that were sick or hurt. In short, she had some kind of "right" to this bird if she so chose. He wasn't the first bird she had requested, but I was deeply reluctant to give up this one.

"But, Alba. I like the way he sings to me."

"No, no. I want bird; you give it to me."

That was that, and Joker went home with her, where he lived with her until she died. It wasn't easy to argue with Alba.

Not that the "bird trade" didn't go in both directions. After Viking, my green-wing macaw, survived the Great Hyacinth Heist, I decided that he was too good to be true and decided to give him to Alba, who had always thought he was special. He is featured in the book *Mrs. Ballard's Parrots,* by Arne Svenson, and lives on in print.

There was also the case of a Moluccan cockatoo named Galaxy who was all feather-plucked and a disaster all around. Alba cured the bird of his plucking and restored him to picture-perfect health. He was beautiful, and she began using him in advertisements and other media. Eventually, the original owners saw their bird on television and sued her, trying to get the bird back. There was a nasty court case, but the judge ruled in Alba's favor and the bird stayed with her. I was her witness in that case, so when I got married a few years later, Galaxy—along with Godfather—witnessed my marriage. Galaxy was dressed up as the bride in a full-length, silk and lace gown, and Godfather as the groom in his black and white tuxedo.

As the years moved on, Alba and I did reach a point where I was no longer allowed in her house. Much as she loved me, my growing business with its increasing number of birds made her concerned that I might bring some evil pathogen into her home and infect her own birds. I became the potential vector, so I was only allowed in the kitchen, where she would still feed me. The downstairs area that housed her flock was now off limits.

When Harry and I appear on *The Martha Stewart Show,* I always think of Alba, who died before she could see me become something of a television personality. After her death from a stroke and subsequent heart attack, her birds were given away piecemeal to various places, and I lost contact with Marvin and Claudio. Shortly after she died, Marvin did return Joker to me. He was all twisted up and crippled from old age, and I kept him until he died three or four years later.

Maybe ten years after she died, I got a call from Arne Svenson, who had been at Elizabeth Taylor's house shortly after Alba died. He had found some old photographs of birds in costumes, photographs Alba had given to Elizabeth. Arne had tracked me down and I was overjoyed to be able to share stories of this brilliant, gifted woman. Eventually, he contacted Marvin and Claudio and then wrote the book, which included many of those photographs.

The book is certainly interesting, but I'm not sure that most readers would realize that Alba's greatest gift to the animal world was her knowledge that lives on through me and in all that I do on behalf of the animals in my life. Before I met her I was like a starving person consuming greasy cheeseburgers, not knowing there is something much more delicious to be had. I literally inhaled her wisdom and filled the void in my own knowledge.

Every Memorial Day, I go to the cemetery where both my grandfather and Alba are buried. I visit their graves, weed the sites, and replace the flowers. I gratefully thank the two people who made me what I am today. I remember that Alba told me if I didn't use my God-given talents to help other people, then something terrible would happen to me. I know she meant it as a "loving curse," because she wanted me to carry on the kind of work she was trying to do—and for which she knew I had a special gift.

CHAPTER 6

A Passion for Birds:
From Front Porch to Penthouse

What fascinates people about parrots, I think, has nothing to do with "flap-flap," but with their beauty and their behavior. Whether it's the crimson, golds, greens, yellows, and blues of the scarlet macaw or the pearly white of the Moluccan cockatoo, their visual appeal is mesmerizing. As companions, they are smart, playful, affectionate, and willful. Parrots can be trained to do tricks or simply to be respectable housemates. They can be caged or uncaged; but they need a habitat that is theirs, where they can toss their food, poop, chew on innumerable toys, sleep, and feel safe. If the bird is caged, it needs time out of the cage to share time with its owner. If the bird is uncaged except for bad-behavior time-outs, then the owner will be forced to make major concessions in his or her home. If the bird lives in an aviary, the owner can visit him there or bring him out to share time with the humans.

There are many who say that parrot keeping is an obsession. Passion for parrot keeping certainly leads to much debate and controversy over what is best and what is right—whether it's food, caging, clipping wings, or free-flighting.

The passion factor is something I have seen firsthand in a wide variety of parrot environments. Perhaps the most spectacular case involved a pair of hyacinth macaws whose acquaintance I made in 1979 in New York City.

Although I was fairly new to the pet business, I had already developed a strong reputation in the greater New York area. One day, I got a call from a gentleman who spoke with what I thought was a Middle Eastern accent. He was in fact Egyptian, his name was Aziz, and he sounded frantic.

"Mr. Morrone, my name is Aziz and I represent a very powerful man who lives here in New York, and also in Saudi Arabia. He has many animals that travel with him to both places. All of his animals are well except for his beloved hyacinth macaws. He is very upset, and is hoping you can help. Will you please come to see what we can do?"

I agreed to go over after I closed my store. Off I went to the east side of Manhattan, where very wealthy people owned many of the town houses. Most of those town houses are five stories tall, often with a penthouse or roof garden and a private garage. I found the address and knocked on the door.

An Egyptian butler greeted me and introduced himself as Aziz. As polite as he was, I hardly noticed him as I stood awestruck by the surroundings. For a moment, I thought I had been transported to a palace in Saudi Arabia. Elaborately embroidered tapestries and Persian rugs adorned the walls and the floors. Ornately carved furniture and an art collection that could have fit in nicely at the Metropolitan seemed right at home with the six saluki hounds that had met me at the door and now followed me around like old friends. Veiled women moved noiselessly around the parlor, their small feet nearly lost in the deep carpets.

Aziz explained that the sheikh did not speak English and he would translate for me. We got into an elevator and went up to the top floor, an atrium with a glass roof and glass walls that opened up to a small garden overlooking the city. Inside the atrium was a long, running perch with three Saker falcons. It was hard to believe I was still in New York. There in the corner was a very large gilded cage with the two hyacinth macaws. The four cage turrets were capped in gold, adding opulence to the environment. And the orchids! I had never seen so many species in such abundance in one space. Everything was absolutely perfect. In sad contrast, the macaws were a wreck.

Their feathers were dried out, their toes were thin, and they were substantially underweight. It made no sense to me that in a house of extreme perfection, these birds could be in such bad shape. I looked at their droppings and saw that by Alba standards, the color and texture were all wrong. Remember that this was 1979 and avian medicine had not yet developed into the science it is today. Diagnosing birds was primarily based on instinct and experience. I observed that the birds didn't have runny noses, and their feathers weren't fluffed up as they would be if the birds had a fever. Perhaps the dishes would tell the story.

The water dish was full of clean, fresh water. This was apparently not a water issue. One of the food dishes was full to the top with gigantic raw peanuts; I had never seen such large peanuts. The other dish was brimming over with enormous black sunflower seeds, each one the size of my thumbnail. I was beginning to see the problem. In South America, wild hyacinth macaws eat Brazil nuts, tiny coconuts, plantains or bananas, and whatever other fruits they can find. As limited as avian knowledge was at the time,

I knew that their diet here in New York was totally wrong for them. The dried feathers also told me that the birds weren't bathing and they weren't being misted, something these birds needed daily.

By contrast, the Saker falcons across the room were in perfect shape, but they were desert birds that didn't require much bathing, and their diet was less variable. This was actually the first time I had ever seen these birds in person. They are common throughout the Middle East, and are used to hunt a particular bird called a houbara. Houbaras are a type of large bustard, a bird that looks like a cross between a turkey and a crane, and were hunted by the sheikh with his falcons and salukis. I had only read about these creatures before, and I was curious.

"Aziz, what does your boss do with the falcons and hounds in Saudi Arabia?"

"He lives there for six months of the year, and he loves to hunt with them while he's there. When the weather becomes too hot, be brings them back to New York, and they live most happily in the house."

I knew that pet birds at that time were allowed to travel between countries as long as they were pets. Birds traveling for commerical purposes needed to be in a thirty-day quarantine. I asked Aziz a few more questions, and then the sheikh, Isa, came in.

He wasn't at all what I had expected (white robes, a meticulously trimmed beard, and older). Isa was a young man, perhaps in his thirties, and was dressed in an expensive-looking suit that said "Wall Street." We shook hands and he explained in broken English that Aziz would translate.

A high-powered Brazilian businessman had made a gift of the macaws, and there was an obviously important but undisclosed relationship between the men. The Brazilian had brought the birds to America and presented them to Isa. Time to ask questions, delicately.

"Please ask Isa what kind of diet he was told to feed them."

A short exchange ensued, and I was beginning to think that there were things about this culture that might require a certain diplomacy in which I might not be versed.

"Isa says that he is feeding the birds exactly what his friend told him. As you see, my boss takes very good care of his animals and orchids. He pays special attention to all species, and is proud of his knowledge and their care. He is giving the birds only the very best sunflower seeds and peanuts as he was instructed to do."

I decided to speak to Aziz in a gentle aside.

"Here's the problem. The birds are getting the wrong diet, and their feathers aren't being misted daily. If he starts to take care of them the correct way, then they'll be fine in a few weeks."

Aziz spoke to me in a way that told me a minefield could be imminent.

"You can't say that the birds are not being well taken care of; it will cause many problems. He will lose face because he prides himself on taking the best possible care of his creatures. His Brazilian friend told him what to feed the birds and that, too, is a problem, because if the Brazilian was wrong about the care of the birds, he might also be wrong about some business matters. That could kill their large international business deal."

"Delicate" seemed to be the order of the day. I needed to think quickly.

"Aziz, what is he supposed to do if the birds get sick?"

He thought for a moment, and it was clear that his brain was racing right alongside mine to come up with a proper solution. Loss of face was at the core of all this.

"Animals and people do get sick. We believe that it is the will of Allah when someone becomes ill, but it is also the will of Allah that man has the knowledge to discover medicines to heal the sickness."

Isa was looking more and more concerned because he was not able to understand what Aziz and I were saying to each other. I looked back at the birds, and suddenly I had an inspiration.

"Aziz, does medicine have to come out of a bottle?"

"No, no. It can come from different sources."

"Okay, get me a pencil and paper."

Within seconds, I had a gold pen in my hand and a pad of paper that looked impressive enough to carry a royal seal.

"I'm ready, Aziz. Let's talk with Isa."

In translation, I first thanked him for inviting me into his home. Then I explained that his birds were sick, I didn't know how they had become sick, and that their sickness was a random event in life. I went on to explain that certain fruits and nuts could cure the sickness, and I would write those down for him. I listed the appropriate foods and the daily amounts, and told him that the proper medicines were in these fruits, nuts, and vegetables. My next inspiration would have made any international negotiator proud. I went on to say that the medicine needed a conduit to go from the bird's body into its feathers; for that, the birds would have to be misted every day. What I knew was that the bird's feather is composed of tiny barbs that hold the composition of the feather.

Those barbs act somewhat like Velcro. When a feather is dry, the barbs disconnect and the feather looks frayed. Once the feather is rehydrated, the birds preen the feather, the barbs become reconnected, and the feather with ratty edges soon becomes fluffy.

"Tell Isa that I will come back in two weeks to check on the birds. I expect that they will be much better by that time."

Isa looked both pleased and relieved. I was ready to leave, but my curiosity about his hunting with falcons made me ask for a small favor.

"Aziz, could you ask Isa to tell me about hunting in Saudi Arabia?"

We all pulled up chairs, and Isa told me all about his adventures—not in Saudi Arabia, as I had presumed, where the sheikhs had hunted the houbara to extinction, but in Pakistan, where the houbara was still common and where they would hunt with their dogs and falcons. It sounded like an exotic safari, searching out the houbara in places that conjure up visions of Osama bin Laden's hiding places. The safaris would be gone for a month at a time. I tried to imagine myself on one of those expeditions, astride an Arabian horse, falcon on my arm, dogs leading the way. At some point, the houbara—which is the heaviest flying bird, nearly thirty pounds—would be dispatched, and there would be a mighty feast with much storytelling and celebrating with exotic teas. Maybe some day . . .

I gave Aziz my phone number and left. Two weeks later I returned as promised and discovered two healthy-looking macaws. Isa offered to pay me a very substantial fee, but I declined. In some small way, I had not only done a good deed, but I had also been able to share vicariously in a lifestyle I could never experience firsthand. Still, Isa was a man of honor.

As I was leaving, he led me into one of the rooms where a carved wooden case stood against one of the tapestried walls. The case was filled with ornately decorated falcon hoods. I had never seen anything like them. Isa opened the case and took out one of the soft, leather hoods. He handed it to me, and Aziz explained that this was a special gift in gratitude for helping him with his birds. I have that hood to this day.

Even now, the picture of that town house with its opulent furnishings, exotic orchids, sleek hounds, falcons, and macaws is a vivid reminder of what ultimate pet keeping looks like. Isa didn't just "own" animals, he created the best life that his wealth could provide for them. Like me, he was a devoted pet keeper.

CHAPTER 7

The Power of the Stoop: Flying with Falcons

My passion for falcons began when I was a small child. The inspiration was a book called *My Side of the Mountain* by Jean Craighead George. It's the story of a boy who runs away from home to live in the Catskill Mountains, where he discovers a peregrine falcon's nest on the side of a cliff. He climbs up to the nest, takes a baby falcon out of the nest, and carries it down with him. He names the bird Frightful and teaches it to hunt for him. I was captivated by the story and decided that someday I, too, would have a falcon. That day came when I was eighteen.

I had to complete substantial paperwork before I could get my first falcon: special permits and licenses, and a test conducted by the Department of Conservation in New York. After securing the permits and licenses, and assuming that I had passed the test, I then had to serve as apprentice to a master falconer. I had no idea where I would find such a sponsor. In the moment, I forgot that Russell Taylor's father might be of help.

As luck would have it, I needed to visit my optometrist, whose office was down the block from my house. He had made my glasses since I was ten, and I mentioned that I hoped to become a falconer and I needed a sponsor.

"I'm a master falconer, Marc."

You could have knocked me over with a falcon feather. My optometrist, Hans Klaasen, who was originally from Holland, had been a falconer in Europe and had become a master falconer in the United States.

"I'd be happy to sponsor you."

Hans knew about my interest in animals, and I couldn't believe my luck in finding a sponsor so easily—and right in my own backyard.

We started my apprenticeship, and I soon learned how to train a bird to fly back to me. Before working with Hans, I had owned birds that would fly to me, but it was always a matter of chance. Now I trained birds to return to me because they wanted to. Contrary to a common misconception, training the bird to return to its owner is not a matter of control. The key is positive reinforcement, and methods using that principle have been passed down from one generation to another for thousands and thousands of years. In fact, falconers with their trained birds of prey were most likely the first pet keepers. Theirs is an art that cannot be learned from any book.

Going back as many as twenty thousand years ago, one has to visualize someone like me wandering through the forest and seeing a goshawk fly down, grab a rabbit, and tussle with it on the ground. That person would have managed to grab both the goshawk and the rabbit, and recognized that he had a choice. He could eat them both or, since he already had a rabbit to eat, he might tie the goshawk's feet together and take it back to his cave or hut, where he could observe it. After a couple of days, he would probably have decided that there wasn't much to do with the hawk, which did nothing but glare at him, so he would have returned to the forest and set it free. Once the hawk had been set loose, and because it hadn't eaten in a couple days, it would likely have landed in a tree and focused its attention on finding another rabbit. Flash! Another rabbit, another catch, and the human would have grabbed them both again. The first falconer was fashioned from mere circumstance.

Someone like me would have said, "I've got to learn more about this." Learning more would have led to a pivotal observation for the future of falconry: "I can train this bird to hunt for me."

Hans explained how birds of prey were trained in Holland and throughout Europe. There were entire families whose job it was to capture falcons and sell them to falconers all over Europe. Most of these early falcon catchers were watchmakers who had small sheds out in the area where the falcons were migrating. Inside the sheds, the falconers worked on their watches. Outside the sheds was an arrangement of nets, and a European bird called a shrike tethered to a perch. When the shrike saw a falcon on the horizon, it would scream, alerting the watchmaker inside that it was time to abandon his watches for the moment. He would open a portal that he could look through. Then he pulled a string that opened a cubbyhole, which in turn opened a little box outside the hut. Inside that box would be a pigeon tied to another string. The falconer manipulated the string so that the pigeon would flutter about and look injured. This attracted the falcon's attention, and it would fly down to grab the pigeon. When it did so, it became caught in the net.

Now the falcon catcher would begin a process called "manning," or "flooding." The process involves staying with the bird twenty-four hours a day. The falconer holds the bird on top of his fist, secured by two leather strings called jesses, which are held tightly inside the trainer's fist so that the bird cannot fly off. The bird comes to believe that no harm will come to it, and that the man's fist is a safe place. Typically, this process takes about two days, but in the falconer's mind, it takes as long as it takes. After the bird has been "flooded" with new information—specifically, that the human will not hurt the bird—it is time to feed the bird. The falconer offers the bird bits of food from his fingers. Eventually, the falconer puts the food on his fist, and the bird becomes comfortable with eating that way. It's important to note that the falcon is not tame; it still has all of its wild instincts. What's gone is the fear. The trained falcon no longer fears humans, and it understands that the human who gives it food is a good thing in its life. Now it's time to fly.

The next step is to take the bird out into the forest and turn it loose. The bird, if it's a hawk, such as a goshawk or red-tailed hawk, will fly up into a tree. Now the bird-human partnership comes into play. The falconer will walk about in search of a squirrel, rabbit, mouse, or vole and try to flush it out. When the bird of prey sees this, it will fly down and grab the animal. The falconer allows the bird to eat as much as it wants and takes the rest home along with the bird. The bird quickly figures out that it can make kills more easily if the human helps out. The falcon, however, hunts in a different manner.

Since most falcons only eat birds, they must catch them on the wing. When a falconer goes hunting with a falcon, he will take it to a field where he knows there are birds hiding—pheasants, ducks, partridges, or quail. The falconer will use a dog to help flush out the birds. The secret to success here is that the falcon has been trained to chase a lure that the falconer spins above his head. When the falcon "catches" the lure, he gets fed. Expecting the lure, the falcon flies up and hovers overhead. Now instead of a lure, there's a real bird, and the catch is accomplished. The falcon folds its wings and descends straight down at a high rate of speed in a movement called the "stoop," snatching and killing the prey in one swift motion. Like the hawk, the falcon quickly determines that the human is an ideal hunting partner. Now the falconer knows that he can release the bird and it will return to him.

When I am going out with my falcon, I first have her chase the lure and I reward her with a little food. Then we go to the car, which she also associates with food because I feed her again when we get there. With the car-food association firmly established, I can arrive at my destination and turn the bird loose for free flight, confident that she will see the car as her "homing device." The bird gets in and out of the car as obligingly as a dog would, and sits comfortably on her perch.

"Free flight" simply means that the bird flies outside, unfettered, and will return to its trainer when called. Years ago, the British lords had their own approach for training their parrots to return. The Duke of Bedford, in particular, hired a gamekeeper to shoot all the hawks, falcons, owls, foxes, weasels, and whatever other predatory animals were on his estate in order to make it safe for his parrots. Then he released his parrots without any worries about their being killed as prey. Given the safety of his estate, and the fact that food was only available back at the house, the parrots associated a round-trip flight with being fed. Most modern parrot owners do not have the luxury afforded to the Duke of Bedford, and the chance of loss is always a reality. I pride myself on free-flighting parrots without losing them, but even I have had my close calls.

One of my favorite parrots to "fly with" is the Patagonian conure, because it's big, has very long wings and tail, and darts and maneuvers like a butterfly. I frequently use these conures for demonstrations to show people how they can free-flight their own birds. For this particular performance at a local fall festival, I practiced the morning of the event in the parking lot behind my store. I was working with a Patagonian conure named Oscar, whose special trick was to sit on my shoulder until I picked him up and threw him up into the air. Up he'd go to a height of fifty or sixty feet, and then he'd zoom back down to my shoulder. I did that over and over again. The bird thought it was a great game, and people found it funny because it looked like I was trying to escape from him.

So there I was, practicing my maneuver, when I realized there was a tension and electricity in the air. I looked over to a group of pigeons that had been feeding in one corner of the parking lot, and suddenly they burst into flight. In the same moment, Oscar flew off my shoulder and circled the parking lot, screaming and screaming. I couldn't grasp what was happening. I watched Oscar circle higher until I saw the source of the pandemonium. It was a peregrine falcon and it was chasing Oscar.

Even though Oscar had been raised in captivity, he somehow

knew that in order to survive he had to fly higher than the falcon. So now I'm watching both birds "ringing up," flying in concentric rings up into the sky until both birds were just dots. The term "ringing up" comes from the way European ladies hunted for skylarks with a type of falcon called a Merlin. While being pursued by the falcon, the skylark would sing loudly as it flew in rings, higher into the sky. Oscar was ringing in order to stay on top, but now suddenly the falcon rose even higher.

The dots moved back into sight, and I saw the falcon close its wings and start to stoop. I thought for sure that Oscar would be killed, but then the conure did something incredibly instinctual— and this by a bird raised in a cage. He waited until just before the falcon hit him, and then he twisted and dipped. Rather than waste energy trying to fly, he stayed in one place, waited until the falcon was directly over him, and then twisted out of the way. The falcon shot right past him, and Oscar flew like an arrow south in a straight line. The falcon now had to come back up out of his stoop, but Oscar's maneuver had bought him time to escape. Both birds were soon out of sight, but five minutes later I saw the falcon fly back and land on the church steeple of a local bell tower, a tower that I would come to know intimately. He was empty-handed, which meant Oscar was probably still alive. Sure enough, someone found Oscar three days later about ten miles south of my store and returned him to me unharmed.

Another falcon encounter with a happy ending involved a street pigeon that I had rescued. The pigeon was a purebred Birmingham Roller, whose method of flying is highly unusual. Unlike homing pigeons that are trained to carry messages, Rollers are trained to fly up in ever-widening rings as high as five hundred feet and then tumble downward, doing backward flips as they fall. "Tumbling" is actually a form of epilepsy, and those who raise Birmingham Rollers measure how far the bird can tumble while in midair. No one knows why the bird doesn't suffer seizures on the ground; it's strictly a midair phenomenon.

It was time to release the Birmingham Roller that I had rescued, and I turned it loose in my parking lot. Instead of flying away in a straight line, it started to ring up, no doubt trying to get its bearings before it flew off. I knew that once it reached the apex of its ring, it would be able to determine how to return home. Just before it reached that apex, I saw what I presumed to be another pigeon flying next to it. It wasn't a pigeon, though; it was a falcon. Apparently, the sight of the falcon next to it caused the pigeon to have a seizure that sent it tumbling downward. The falcon was only able to make a small strike, and I could see the puff of white feathers from where I stood. Down the bird tumbled, and I knew that if I didn't somehow catch it, the bird would crash to the ground and die. I quickly pulled out my shirt and began my "Barney Rubble" routine, running about to position myself for the big catch. Thump! The little pigeon landed safely in my shirt, and I took it back to my store, where it could recover. A couple of weeks later, I released it without incident.

With any luck, there wouldn't be another falcon in its future.

. ˙. .

Since childhood, whether I am reading a book or out in the forest with my falcon, Bubbles, or performing duties as a master bander, falcons continue to be a major part of my life. My favorite falcons to band are peregrines, and I've had many adventures doing so. The reason I, or anyone else, bands a falcon is to be able to track its flyway patterns. Knowledge of the patterns is essential in order to preserve habitats and understand more about the nature of these magnificent birds. I consider the falcon to be a perfect creature, and I am proud to be a master falconer and a master bander.

The process for banding involves setting up a hut on the south shore of Long Island, along one of the barrier beaches. In front of my blind I tether a pigeon to one string and a starling to another. These are my "bait" birds, and I've been using the same birds for the past twelve years. In front of the bait birds is a triangle of nets called mist nets. I'm facing north while the birds are migrating south. I always do this in the fall, which is peak migration time.

So I sit there, and I watch and I watch and I watch. Incoming falcons come in for the bait and become entangled in the nets that in no way hurt them. I disentangle the bird, measure and weigh it, put on a dated band, and then set it free. Typically, this routine plays out over and over again without incident. My biggest fear is deer.

If a deer runs into my nets, it will ruin them. These nets are very expensive, and when I hear a sudden crack or crunching sound, I'm on full alert.

Uh-oh.

The nearby crack of a branch told me a deer was standing directly in front of the nets. If I put my hand out of the blind and waved, the deer might move to the right or left and safely away from the nets. No such luck. With one awkward jump, the deer landed smack in the middle of my nets. I watched as the entangled deer bounded away across the meadow and then collapsed next to the road. I ran across the meadow, hoping that no one on the road would see the deer all tangled up. Fortunately, the deer was a doe, so I didn't have antlers to deal with, but she was big and so were her hooves. Without even thinking about the danger, I jumped on top of her and ripped the net, which came off easily. The deer ran off unhurt. Only one net had been ruined and I went back to the blind to survey the others. The banding spot was now in a state of devastation. The two remaining nets were on the ground covered in weeds and stickers, and I had no choice but to clean them. The nets used by banders are incredibly fine and nearly invisible, so debriding the nets was no easy task. After an hour, I decided it was time to return to the store, and I started to gather up my gear.

Whoosh! Right into one of the nets came one of the biggest peregrine falcons I'd ever encountered. I rushed over and picked her up and was struck by the number of bands on her legs. I'd never seen so many bands on one bird, and the story they told was no less amazing. Each band represented a chapter in her life. The bird had been bred in captivity at a facility of the Peregrine Foundation in Iowa and then purchased by the city council in Toronto, when it was still a baby. The bird had been "hacked out," or raised without parents, in a natural area so that it would be able to imprint in the wild when it was grown. When it reached maturity, it flew away and ended up in Maine, where someone else banded it. Then the bird flew to me. I could tell by its weight that it was well fed, so I knew that it was living a successful wild life. That bird became part of my records, along with every other bird I have ever banded. Banding isn't just about flyway patterns; it's also about recognizing birds as individuals.

Banding isn't the only way to be close to falcons. The bell tower incident was a clear reminder that unlike falcons, I don't have wings.

I was in search of a peregrine falcon nest thought to be located in the bell tower of St. Agnes Cathedral, one of the tallest buildings on the south shore of Long Island. First, I had to get special permission from the church, which I managed to do by presenting a letter from the Department of Conservation. Off I went to the cathedral, where I found myself in the company of the janitor who was to accompany me up to the bell tower, along with the biologist from the Department of Conservation. We climbed six flights of stairs until we were at the tower itself. In order to get up to the tower, I had to climb a ladder. The "ladder" that climbed another hundred feet was nothing more than metal spikes sticking out of the brick wall. The janitor was a very large man, and I had concerns about his climbing ahead of me. The biologist would also join us. I did not want to be last, because if either man fell backward, I'd be knocked off the ladder.

"Why don't I go first?"

The janitor agreed, and up the three of us went. When we reached the top, we went through a trapdoor before we could finally get inside the bell tower. The tower is over a hundred years old and the bell is no longer there, having been replaced by an electronic system. Hexagon-shaped, the tower had six small stained-glass windows in each of the walls. Only one of the windows opened, and I was the only one skinny enough to climb through.

I squeezed out of the window and found myself standing on a ledge that was only two feet wide and what seemed like a million miles from the ground. I felt like Spider-Man, but without that good, sticky stuff on my hands and feet.

What in the world am I doing?

The wind was blowing, and I expected to be swept off the ledge at any moment.

I'm getting out of here. I'm climbing back inside.

That was when I saw hundreds of bird wings on the ledge. The naturalist in me overwhelmed the skinny guy and I had to study these. There were wings of robins, cardinals, mallard ducks, teal ducks, pigeons, and woodpeckers, so many species. I stuffed handfuls inside the window, knowing that the biologist would be equally amazed. I had had no idea that the diet of a peregrine falcon was so varied. Most people presume a pigeon diet. Who would have imagined a peregrine falcon catching and eating a downy woodpecker?

Now, I was convinced there must be a nest around one of these corners. Like Lucy pretending to be Superman in one of my favorite episodes of *I Love Lucy,* I inched around the ledge, bending down to collect wings as I went. I ended up at the original window where I had climbed out, but no nest. The biologist and I decided that this was only a feeding station. A nest would never survive on such a narrow ledge.

"Well, Marc, what do you think about putting a nesting box up here?"

I don't think so.

Give me the little blind on the barrier beach, where I can sit in silence and observe clouds of swallows eating waxberries, so uncharacteristic of their insect-eating habits. Where one moment I can watch red foxes come within a few feet of my blind, and in the next observe a great blue heron, in stark contrast to its fish-eating ways, swoop down from the sky to catch a starling on the beach. Where I can watch flocks of migrating warblers and flickers, grazing deer, and a host of other animals, all within view of my tent.

Perfect contentment with my band of brothers.

PART II

A PET IN EVERY PORT

CHAPTER 8

Passports for Pooches and Pets

Becoming an animal exporter was never part of my original plan. It all began innocently enough with a letter that showed up randomly in my mail back in 1988. I had been in business since 1978, when I opened my first store in Rockville Centre. The letter was from a man named Mr. Kamiya in Japan who owned a company called Pet Forest. He wanted to know if I could send him four parrots.

I had no idea how to send birds to a foreign country, so I had to do prodigious research about what was involved. I quickly learned that any animal that lives wild anywhere in the world, and that is to be exported from the United States, must have a permit issued by the U.S. Fish and Wildlife Service. That's because certain animals are protected under what's called CITES, or the Convention for International Trade in Endangered Species. Even if that animal is now commonly kept as a pet, if it is considered endangered within its native habitat, it cannot be exported unless there is verification that it was bred in captivity from ancestors who were legally acquired in the country of origin. The African Grey parrot is a good example. If I have a bird whose bred-in-captivity history goes back several generations, I have to be able to verify that its original, imported ancestor was legally acquired from West Africa. CITES then endorses the legality of the intended export. In addition, the exporter has to produce certain health papers that are only issued by the Department of Agriculture. This applies to any animal that is exported from the United States, not just birds.

After I had learned all that I needed to know in order to ship those four parrots to Mr. Kamiya, I had my first conversation with him.

"Mr. Kamiya, I'm just curious how you happened to choose me. I didn't realize my name was known in Japan."

"I didn't know your name. I was recently in New York and looked through the Yellow Pages for someone who handled parrots. I figured that someone who owned a store called Parrots of the World could get birds sent to me in Japan."

"Well, I'm really glad you did, and I've done all the research on how to get those birds shipped to you. I've always admired how well the Japanese people take care of their pets."

The birds arrived safely in Japan, and I felt encouraged to pursue more exporting. Foreign buyers can afford to pay top prices for exported animals, and that would certainly help my pet store business, the income of which was highly variable. How to start?

I contacted my art dealer friend who was also a good customer, because I knew he had an art gallery in Tokyo.

"Hi, John, it's Marc. Listen, I really want to do more exporting to Japan. Do you think you could have one of your gallery employees in Tokyo go out and buy a couple of pet magazines and send them to me?"

This was 1988 and I didn't know of anyone else in the United States who was exporting animals to Japan.

"Sure, Marc."

A month later, two magazines showed up in the mail, one called *Anifa* and one called *All Birds*. The magazines looked fascinating, but they were of course all in Japanese. Aha! One of my employees was of Japanese descent, and his mother spoke Japanese fluently.

She very kindly translated both magazines, and we decided to start with a company called Asada Choju Trading Company. *Choju* is the Japanese word for animal, and Asada was the name of the woman who owned the company. Mrs. Asada is the most respected animal person in Japan.

With my translator's help, we called up Mrs. Asada late one night, New York time, and we asked if she might want to buy some ferrets. I had a good instinct that ferrets would be good pets for Japanese people living in small apartments, and I knew that Wendy Winstead could help me with the breeding side. I had offered ferrets to Mr. Kamiya, but he hadn't been interested. Mrs. Asada was, and I was up and running.

For her first order, Mrs. Asada wanted ferrets, hedgehogs, and a few parrots. All the animals arrived safely; she sold those, and ordered more. At one point I was sending her a hundred ferrets a week, along with other species, and my name started to become well known all over Japan. Now I had even more customers, and then my reputation spread to Korea, Taiwan, Singapore, and other parts of Asia. Today, I export animals all over the world. The list includes Mexico, Panama, Costa Rica, Guatemala, Venezuela, Brazil, Argentina, Chile, Canada, Norway, Iceland, Denmark, Germany, France, England, Switzerland, Russia, Spain, Portugal, Italy, Malta, Turkey, Pakistan, Kenya, South Africa, Malaysia, Singapore,

Thailand, Korea, Mainland China, Taiwan, Japan, Australia, Dubai, Kuwait, United Arab Emirates, and a couple of others I'm probably forgetting.

Needless to say, adventures abound in the export business.

There was the case of a dog I needed to send to Macao, which at the time was a city off the coast of China and independent from the mainland. Asian airlines like China Airlines or Air China didn't fly there at all. The only way to fly there was to fly to Taiwan and then take additional flights to get to Macao. An American businessman who'd been transferred there wanted me to ship his dog to him. Mmm. Problematic. Flying the dog through Taiwan meant too many layovers for the dog; that wouldn't work.

I did my research and discovered that Macao was actually a Portuguese colony.

Ah, I thought to myself. *I bet the Portuguese people must be able to fly direct to Macao.* So I called a Portuguese airline, and sure enough, they did. Now, all I had to do was ship the dog to Lisbon; and it would only have to stay in Lisbon for two hours before it was on the next plane to Macao. Everything went as planned, and the dog was reunited with its owner.

Sleuthing is a big part of making the export business work, that and a lot of ingenuity. Different cultures place different values on certain animals. The Chinese, Guyanese, and Mediterranean cultures love their singing birds. East Indians revere and protect their cows. Saudi Arabians value their dogs insofar as they are "useful"—police dogs, guard dogs, and seeing-eye dogs. A potential culture clash came about when a company here in New York asked me to export a Lhasa apso belonging to one of their executives who was being transferred to Saudi Arabia. The dog was considered a member of the family, and it was essential that the dog live with him and his family in their new home. Knowing what I did about Saudi Arabian culture and "useful" dogs, the Lhasa apso was going to be a challenge, because the Saudi government would see him merely as a "pet."

I went to my friend Roger Caras, who at the time was president of the American Kennel Club, and asked his advice. Quoting from a respected canine document, Roger provided me with the proof of lineage for the breed. Lhasas are descended from Tibetan guard dogs, and by definition are "guard" dogs. While I certainly can't imagine this diminutive animal protecting a household from some burly intruder, its proof of lineage was enough for the Saudis, and off it went to live happily ever after in Saudi Arabia. Aside from its AKC papers, the little dog now had a special badge as a "useful" guard dog.

Along with this and many other adventures, I quickly became a world-respected exporter, and I would get calls from all over the world requesting a wide variety of animals. Pigeons, in particular, are still one of the most common animals that I ship overseas. Not too long ago, I got a call from a gentleman in New York City who wanted me to send a few fancy pigeons to his boss in Saudi Arabia.

"Sure, I can do that." I didn't see any difficulty in shipping pigeons to Saudi Arabia. It had to be easier than shipping parrots to Japan.

"You see, Mr. Morrone, the paperwork is very difficult to get."

"Don't worry; I love challenges."

"Good, good. My boss is in New York right now, and he would like to meet you."

"Of course. Have him come in whenever he wants to."

When Tarik Saedii arrived in my store, he was not the "sheikh" I expected. He looked more like Isa on Park Avenue. He explained that he had acquired some pigeons at a pigeon show here in the States and needed someone to arrange for their shipment back to his home. I assured him that I could handle this, and off he went, satisfied that his birds would be able to fly back to his home in the Middle East.

I immediately went to my favorite veterinarian, who needed to examine the pigeons and fill out certain forms. The hard part would be persuading the Department of Agriculture to stamp those forms and then having them approved by the Saudi Arabian consulate. The forms had to be stamped on a particular day at a particular time. I crossed every t and dotted every i, and the birds were shipped successfully.

Fortunately, my attention to detail paid off, and when the birds arrived at the airport in Saudi Arabia, there was a big celebration at the airport, and afterward my export business to the Middle East exploded.

Sometimes, my export business surprises me in other ways.

"Are you the gentleman who's the expert at shipping pigeons around the world?"

The accent was thickly Irish. At the time, Ireland was not on my roster of exporting expertise.

"Yes, I am."

I wasn't being arrogant. My confidence was based on experience.

"Oh, that's so wonderful. Could you give us directions to your store? We'll be coming from New Jersey, and we're in a terrible fix."

Again, the man who walked through the door wasn't exactly who I expected.

Jim was a short, swarthy man with very large forearms. He looked a little like Popeye and struck me as someone who had done intense manual labor all of his life.

"Are you Marc?"

We shook hands, and he began to unfold his tale of woe.

"Well, you see, I'm Jim from Dublin and we're in a terrible fix. Me and my friends, we took all of our life savings and came to the United States to buy these special pigeons. Mr. Morrone, we invested everything we have in these birds, and now we're not able to take them back with us. We don't know who can help us, or how to get the necessary papers to ship them. Here, we have all of our birds in these cardboard boxes, and we don't know what to do."

Jim was soon joined by five enormous guys, big, red-faced Irishmen twice his size. And they looked very upset.

"Don't worry, gentlemen, I can handle this. First, let's get the pigeons taken care of. I have an empty loft downstairs."

We all went downstairs to where I had my pigeon lofts, and fortunately one of them was empty. We unloaded the birds and watched them get happy—drinking water, eating food, and chasing one another all around. Suddenly, I heard all this sniffing behind me and turned to see six Irishmen, who could have picked me up and broken me in two, in tears.

I didn't get it. "What's the matter?"

"Oh, we're just so relieved that you're saving our birds, and all our life's savings."

"Not a problem. I'll get your birds home to you."

With that, the biggest guy got down on his knees and grabbed my hand.

"I just want to thank you from the bottom of my heart."

I was so touched by all of this sentiment. The men left, the birds were shipped; and back home the men bred some excellent birds that won them prizes and made back all the money they had invested, plus more. That was fifteen years ago; and every year, Jim comes back to the United States to buy more pigeons, and I ship his pigeons back to him in Ireland. He has also become one of the most respected pigeon judges in the world and travels all over for shows. Someday, I hope to be able to travel to one of those shows and see Jim in action.

Exporting has opened my eyes to cultures I might never have experienced firsthand. Beyond any commercial benefit, the deepest rewards are definitely to be found in the human-animal connection. Without my export business, I would not be a true "citizen of the world."

CHAPTER 9

Porcupines Arriving at Gate 9

ultural exposure aside, the export business is never without a sense of adventure. Most of those adventures start with a phone call.

This call was from a man I'd known twenty years earlier. He had just imported four African crested porcupines from Guinea-Bissau, and he needed my help. Most people probably think porcupines are from North America, but there are also arboreal porcupines that live in South America and larger, terrestrial porcupines that live in Africa. North American porcupines have spines with little hooked barbs at the tip, whereas the porcupines in Africa have sharp barbs with no hook at the tip. They're also much larger than their North American relatives. Those giant crested types stand as high as a tall man's knee. The spines of a porcupine are actually modified hairs, and the animal grows new ones to replace any spines they lose when they hit someone with their tail. They don't really throw their spines, which are loosely connected to the skin and which will easily lodge in another animal's skin.

Something else many people don't know is that porcupines are not related to the hedgehogs that we keep as pets, and which are also originally from Africa. Porcupines are from the rodent family, and hedgehogs are insectivores like shrews and moles. Unlike the porcupine, which will use his tail as a defensive weapon, the hedgehog will roll into a ball, protected by the spines around its body. Hedgehogs here in the United States have been domesticated for many years, and I sell them as pets in my store.

Back to my call: this acquaintance from Tennessee wanted me to go to the airport and fix a problem with his shipment. The box in which porcupines had been shipped wasn't strong enough, and the big rodents had chewed their way out of it. The animals were running all over the airport, and he needed me to capture and rebox them so that they could be shipped to him in Tennessee. He had arranged to resell them to a zoo in his state, and he was frantic over their escape.

I prepared a couple of sturdy boxes lined with wire and sheet metal, and off I went to the airport. I had no idea how I was going to catch these African crested porcupines. I didn't even know if they were full-grown or just babies, so I also took a big fishing net, just in case. When I got to Kennedy Airport, I went straight to the hangar, where the cargo workers were standing around with puzzled looks on their faces.

"Where are the porcupines?"

More puzzled looks, and they jerked their thumbs toward the warehouse. I walked inside, alone, but didn't see anything. Then I heard this strange rattling noise. Suddenly, a porcupine came zooming out from behind a box. The rattling noise was the sound his spines made when they rubbed against one another. It was an incredibly loud noise, much to my surprise.

I ran after the porcupine, amazed that he could run as fast as I could. It was all I could do to keep up with him in the giant warehouse. Finally, I caught up with him. He'd left his mark; my pants and shoes were covered in quills. At least he hadn't bitten me. African porcupines have huge orange teeth that are like chisels. They're orange from all the gnawing they do. So before he could either bite me or run away, I scooped him up and popped him into the box. One down, three to go.

The second was only a baby, and I easily picked him up with one hand. Two more to go, both adults. Again, a merry chase with my trying to keep up with them. North American porcupines are slow and lumbering, nothing like these distant relatives. Finally, I caught up with them, and into the boxes they went. My legs were once again covered in quills, but they hadn't gone in that deeply and I was able to pull them out. Had they reached my skin, it would have been a very different story.

Now that the animals had been reboxed, they were ready to be shipped the next day. They arrived safely in Tennessee, and I never heard from my friend again. Not even a thank you.

What I still remember most about my adventure with these African porcupines is the name they've been given in their native land. The pidgin name for them is "chook chook beef." "Beef" is the universal word in that language for animal, and I figured the "chook" part probably came from the sound they make when they run. It's not. "Chook" is the native word for a doctor's hypodermic needle, which resembles the spines. The pidgin way of pluralizing a word is to repeat it, thus "chook chook." The porcupines are also considered a delicacy in West Africa.

No cook cook the chook chook.

CHAPTER 10

All Ferrets Aboard!

While porcupines may be prickly, the soft, friendly ferret is one of my favorite animals. Contrary to what many people might think, ferrets are not rodents and they do make wonderful pets. As members of the weasel family, ferrets are related to skunks, minks, and otters, with whom they share one distinctive characteristic: a scent gland that needs to be removed in order to avoid smell issues. All ferrets bred and sold here in the United States have had that gland removed and are neutered. They're cuddly and cute and enjoy interacting with humans.

They also appear on television and in movies. The other night I was watching the HBO series called *Big Love,* and to my surprise there was a scene with ferrets. A couple was sitting in the park, petting two ferrets, while another woman looked on in horror.

"Oh, no, look at those horrible people petting their rats!"

In the background, the ferrets were making little squeaking noises while they were being petted. I laughed out loud. Ferrets are basically mute; the only sounds they make are tiny, nearly inaudible grunts or a high scream when they are scared. Ferrets in movies or on television are always dubbed. Quiet is another positive aspect of ferrets as pets.

That rodent misconception and prejudice has led municipalities like New York City and California to make owning a ferret illegal. As a pet keeper and exporter, I provide ferrets to people all over the world, especially Japan. I've also owned ferrets, and I regard them as one of the best pets available.

Small enough to hold in your arms, ferrets are indeed cuddly and affectionate. They're also optimistic creatures that greet each day with enthusiasm. When you want to play with one, it responds with a look that says, "Hooray, I get to play!" When you need to put it back in its cage, it goes back without any objection and promptly takes a nap. Ferrets sleep eighteen hours a day, so spending time in a cage isn't a problem for them. In fact, ferrets really do need to spend considerable time in their cages, not just because they sleep, but also because the cage is their litter box. The ferret's digestive system is very, very fast; whatever they eat is gone twenty minutes later. A ferret loose in the house will convert your house into a giant litter box. It isn't that they're dirty; they prefer to eliminate in one place. But if that one place is too far away and nature calls, the ferret will answer, wherever he is. Ferrets are also very curious animals, another reason for them to be kept in cages. A ferret will crawl into any space where its head can fit, and it will hide whatever it finds.

Feeding a ferret is a simple matter. There's a special dry ferret food designed for their optimal health. That said, it's also true that they don't live long, somewhere between six and eight years for most. Of course, one of my own ferrets, Jingles, lived to be twelve. There's a miracle for sure. When he was young, one of my wolves got hold of him, gave him a nasty shake, and literally broke his back. For four months, Jingles' back legs were paralyzed and it was heartbreaking to watch him. Somehow, I knew he would not only survive but thrive. Slowly, his nerves regenerated, and he resumed bouncing around like the happy ferret he was.

In terms of domestication, ferrets are one of man's best accomplishments. Ferrets have been kept as pets for thousands of years, often used in ferreting, which is actually hunting for rabbits. In Europe, hunters would go out with a ferret, a dog, and a hawk in search of a rabbit warren. Unlike American rabbits in the wild, European rabbits still have a very complex social and living structure; it's not a matter of a rabbit under this bush or behind that thicket. "Ferreting out" a rabbit takes skill. The first thing the hunter does is to net as many of the warren holes as he can, leaving one hole open for the ferret to enter. Down goes the ferret, and now rabbits start to pop up out of any open holes they can find, where they are caught in the nets. The dog, called a lurcher, is a cross between a greyhound and a terrier, so it's very fast. The dog goes after the rabbits on the ground that have escaped from the nets. The hawk, usually a Harris hawk, attacks stragglers from the air. Ferrets are excellent team players.

Here in the United States, as well as in Japan, ferrets have only been raised as pets for the past thirty-five years or so. The person responsible for introducing them to us and to the rest of the world was Wendy Winstead. In many ways she changed the entire world for ferrets. Sadly, she died young of ovarian cancer and didn't live to see the fruits of her hard labor.

Back thirty-five years ago, Wendy was a medical student in New York City who kept skunks as pets. When one of her skunks died, she decided to get a ferret because it was a relative of the skunk. The only reason ferrets had not become popular as pets was because of their scent gland; otherwise they were perfectly domesticated. Wendy got two ferrets and had them both neutered. Female ferrets are especially prone to all sorts of medical problems, so spaying is important for the animal's health. She also had their scent glands removed. She then discovered what wonderful pets they made, and she began to show them around to her friends. It wasn't long before she found her way to *The Late Show with David Letterman*, and the ferret frenzy was full on. She went back to the ferret farm where she'd bought her ferrets and bought more. Now the starving medical student was selling ferrets and doing quite well. It wasn't long before I heard about her, and the next thing we knew we were in the ferret business together.

The ferret bandwagon hit big, and other related industries began springing up across the country. Ferret food, ferret toys, even ferret clothing became a worldwide, billion-dollar industry. Wendy never got to see how big ferrets became, but she certainly created an ongoing pet phenomenon.

Another significant ferret friend was and still is Michael Coleman. I first met him in the early days of exporting ferrets to Japan, where Michael had moved after having been stationed there with the Marines. He shared my "love" for ferrets and was my biggest competitor at the time. One thing led to another, and we decided to work together instead of against each other. He still lives in Japan, and he is highly regarded by both Japanese buyers and Americans.

Not everyone is a ferret enthusiast. New York City and California, as mentioned, have made owning ferrets illegal. In California, especially, the Department of Fish and Game is vigilant about ferret keeping, fearful that pet ferrets will escape and breed in the wild. Impossible. All ferrets bred and sold in this country are neutered before they're sold. Nonetheless, California is adamant about them. Here in the city of New York, ferrets are also illegal but the laws are not so strictly enforced.

In contrast to some people here in the United States, the Japanese are crazy for ferrets. Living space is at premium in Japan, and most people live in small apartments that are perfect for keeping ferrets as pets.

It's not just about keeping their ferrets comfortable and cuddling with them; the Japanese also have elaborate ferret festivals, often held on big hotel rooftops. There's no competition involved, not like the Chinese with their finches or the Middle Easterners with their pigeons. These festivals are all about fun and creating a venue for people to share their ferrets with other like-minded enthusiasts.

In a typical event, hundreds of owners will show up and work their way around what amounts to a "play circuit." First, there might be a "sumo wrestling" ring where a bunch of ferrets all wrestle with one another. Ferrets love to do that, and the last ferret in the ring wins. Another game might be "tube running," where ferrets run through long flexible tubing. The fastest ferret through the tube is the victor. The Japanese also dress up their ferrets in costumes with prizes for the best ones. Those ferrets look remarkably like the *anime* characters found in *manga* literature.

All of the ferrets in Japan are exported from the United States, and Michael Coleman and I are their major suppliers. I also export ferrets to Europe, and a recent shipment bound for Frankfurt nearly became an international event.

A buyer in Holland wanted me to export three hundred ferrets for one of his customers in Frankfurt. That's a huge number of ferrets to ship. It means thirty boxes of ferrets, ten baby ferrets to each box. This was December, and his customer wanted his ferrets in time for Christmas.

I carefully prepared the shipping boxes, which are roomy and well ventilated, and got the ferrets boxed in time for a holiday delivery. The buyer in Holland had instructed me to send the animals to an agent in Frankfurt, but he had mistakenly given me the address for an agent in Brussels. I filled out all the paperwork and delivered the ferrets to the airline for shipping. I postponed a business trip to Wisconsin until the next day, so that I could be sure the ferrets had arrived safely.

As soon as I knew the ferrets had landed in Belgium, I took off for Wisconsin. I was barely under way when I got a call on my cell phone, and my export "ESP" said this was not a good call. Having never before shipped ferrets to Belgium, I had no idea they were illegal there; and no one had flagged my paperwork here in the United States. Now these weary travelers would have to come all the way back.

Shipping back three hundred ferrets. What a nightmare!

Unfortunately, the ferrets had landed in Brussels on a Friday, and there were no flights coming back to the United States on Saturday. So now the ferrets had to be taken out of their boxes and delivered to the animal holding area in the airport. The plan was to repack the ferrets on Sunday and ship them back to me.

Then another ominous phone call.

"The ferrets are all dead."

In desperation, I called a friend of mine who happened to live in Belgium and asked him to drive to the airport and see what had happened. Because ferrets are not kept as pets in Belgium, no one knows anything about them, and my friend arrived to find three hundred very still ferrets, heads back and mouths open. One of the attendants picked up one of the babies, and it just lay there limp in his hand. My friend looked at the ferret and calmly said, "They're just sleeping."

My friend knew that when ferrets sleep they look dead. Even if you prod them or pick them up while they're asleep, they will stay sound asleep. It takes three or four minutes for the ferret to wake up, so now the attendants had to go around waking up all of the sleeping animals. Then it was time to repack them, and back came the ferrets to me.

I picked them up at the airport, brought them back to the pet store, cleaned their boxes, gave them fresh food and water, and gave them a chance to rest before they flew east again. Then it was back to the airport, and off they went to become Christmas presents. This time they arrived safely in Frankfurt, and everyone who was gifted with a ferret sang "Deck the Halls."

Ferrets aren't only perfect pets, they're hardy.

CHAPTER 11

Splash!

Traveling is something my favorite ferret, Splash, did very well. On one occasion, he took an unscheduled walkabout and ended up saving his own life.

I was scheduled to do a cable television show the Wednesday before Thanksgiving. This was a live show and there were animals loose all over the set. When the show was over, I gathered up everyone to go home, but Splash was nowhere to be found. Ferrets are small and skinny, so he could have been hiding anywhere. We looked all over the studio, desperate to find him before the studio closed. That was a big issue because I wouldn't be able to go back the next day and look. Not only would the studio be closed for Thanksgiving, it would also be closed until the following Monday. Finally, we all had to leave—without Splash—so the best I could do was leave behind his carrier with a bowl of food and some water. I knew he'd pop up somewhere, but where? If he somehow got outside, then what? I was brokenhearted to think that I might lose him forever.

Driving home, all I could think about was Splash.

"He's gone; he's gone. I'll never have another ferret like Splash."

I thought of his cute face with the splash of white down the front. That's why I'd named him Splash. What made him so special, though, was that he wouldn't hurt birds. Ferrets have a thing for birds, not a good thing. Ferrets are fine with dogs and cats but given the opportunity, they'll go after birds. Splash got along fine with all of my birds, so I was able to use him in my television menagerie without worrying about them. His playful personality also added tremendously to the synergy of the menagerie.

Just before I arrived home, my cell phone rang and it was my wife.

"Marc, they found Splash. The editor who found him is waiting for you at his home."

"Who found him?" The pounding rainstorm was making it difficult to hear. I also didn't remember seeing anyone else in the studio when I left.

I reached the editor's home in less than half an hour, and there was the editor with Splash resting comfortably in his cage. Both looked relieved.

"My car was the last one left in the parking lot. It's a long way to where it was parked in the middle of the lot, so I ran because of the rain. I'm opening the door when I feel a tug on my pants leg. There he was, tugging away. So I picked him up and put him in my car while I went back to the studio to get his carrier."

I couldn't believe it. In the first place, how had Splash even gotten out of the studio? And how did he know to walk all the way over to the only car in the parking lot, a car belonging to the only human being left on the premises? Ferrets are slow-moving animals; they don't cover long distances well. What could have made him walk all that distance toward an object he didn't even recognize? It was indeed a miracle.

Our next encounter with fate had nothing to do with miracles, and everything to do with wits. As I said before, ferrets have been and still are illegal in New York City; however, from time to time, there were people who tried to get the law changed. One especially passionate city official contacted me and offered to help.

"I just don't understand, Marc, why they're illegal. They're so sweet, and they're perfect for New York City apartments. I have an idea."

Her idea was to hold a press conference, and create a dialogue about ferrets as pets. She wanted me to be part of it, and of course I agreed. Mayor Giuliani wasn't at all pleased, and he ordered the police department to arrest anyone with a ferret and confiscate the animal. No one had told me about this; and I happily climbed into the limousine sent by the city official, carrying me, my macaw Harry, and Splash.

Minutes away from the event, I got a call from one of my friends who knew I would be arriving with a ferret.

"Marc, did you bring Splash?"

Mary was more than a friend. She and her husband, Eric, owned *Modern Ferret* magazine, and they were already at the conference.

"Sure. Of course I brought Splash."

"You can't. The mayor has instructed both the Police Department and the Health Department to confiscate any ferret that shows up."

"Okay, okay, thanks so much. I'll figure something out."

The clock was ticking, and I could already see what looked like at least twenty policemen positioned by the entrance to the conference. Thinking fast, I called back Mary and told her to meet me around the corner from the event. I tapped the driver on the shoulder.

"Sir, don't stop in front of the building. Drive around the corner instead. Thanks."

My two friends were waiting, and I handed them the carrier with Splash inside.

"Thanks again for the heads up. Here's Splash. Take the train back to Rockville Centre and my wife will meet you at the pet store."

I said good-bye to Splash, and back into the limo I went. Now it was just Harry and me, but nobody else knew that. I turned his carrier so that you couldn't see what was inside. When I got out of the car, what looked like forty policemen began walking toward me. I'm sure someone had told them that I'd be arriving with a forbidden ferret.

"Mr. Morrone, would you please put down that carrier so we can look inside."

"Not a problem, officer."

With that, I set down the carrier and opened it up. Out came Harry, and up he went on my shoulder, ready for the show. The officers looked inside the carrier, convinced that a "rodent" must be hidden in there somewhere. When they didn't find anything, they let me pass, and I walked up the stairs, bird in hand and "bird" in the bush. The event attracted considerable attention for the status of ferrets; but ultimately, City Hall won. Even though the good city official did manage to get a law passed to make ferrets legal, the mayor vetoed it at the last minute, asserting that he had to support the findings of the Health Department. Ferrets were still illegal, but there was an interesting twist to the outcome.

At the time, there was a passionate ferret supporter out on Long Island, and he was determined to speak with the mayor about the issue. Giuliani had a live radio show every weekend, where he invited people to call in and share their views and concerns. This supporter became well known to the operators who put through the calls, and the mayor made sure this "ferret fanatic" didn't get on the air. Mistakes will happen, though, and one weekend ferrets hit the air—and the fan. In truth, Giuliani was both polite and sympathetic to the man, but a couple of news agencies who heard the exchange put a different spin on it. The mayor was portrayed as having been rude and having "tortured" his listener, which wasn't true, but that became a media brouhaha. He may have won the war, but the ferrets scored one little victory.

CHAPTER 12

Will Park Your Pigeons . . .
and Your Car

In contrast to the Japanese, who embrace their ferrets with great affection, Americans and pigeons have a much different relationship. Here in New York there are three primary pigeon images that come to mind for most people.

First, there's the sweet, older woman sitting on a park bench, tossing food to the hungry pigeons gathered around her feet. If the weather is good, the pigeons get fed. If the weather is bad, and the woman isn't there, they go hungry. If the woman is there, and a dog chases them, they don't get fed, either. In the sweetest of ways, pigeons—like all birds—accept the random nature of their food supply, and indeed of their life.

The second image most New Yorkers and other city dwellers have of pigeons is of overhead bombardiers. A third common image is of the homing pigeon that delivers messages and manages to find its way home again.

What many people may not realize is that for many cultures throughout the world, pigeons are highly prized as pets or simply for their beauty. Pigeons breed very quickly. Ten generations of pigeons can be produced in only five years. A breeder can thus create his own special line and breed for a particular standard. From muffled tumblers with big, feathery muffs on their feet to Birmingham Rollers that can be bred to tumble in midair, pigeons offer countless possibilities for pet keepers, breeders, and exporters.

In 2002, a major explosion in demand for pigeons occurred both here and abroad, especially by buyers from the Middle East. That year, one of the biggest pigeon shows in the world was held in Pennsylvania. I had no idea it was being held so close to New York, and then suddenly I started getting all these phone calls from people with heavy accents asking directions to our store. All day long it was "directions" and more "directions." Then people started showing up.

The first was a gentleman from Saudi Arabia and he was carrying a box with fifty pigeons in it. He set the box down and pulled out a piece of paper. He couldn't speak English, but he could write English. He wrote down that he was a doctor from Saudi Arabia, that he had bought these pigeons from the show, and that he needed me to ship them home. I agreed, in writing, and he and I went downstairs to put the pigeons in one of the lofts. We went back upstairs, and there was another Saudi gentleman who spoke no English but who could write, and he also had a box of pigeons with him. Back downstairs, unload more pigeons, and back upstairs to find three more gentlemen with boxes of birds. Some were from Saudi Arabia, others from Qatar, Bahrain, and Kuwait.

All day long, boxes of pigeons and people who could only write English continued to arrive. The lofts were soon full, so now I had pigeons in parakeet cages, rabbit cages, dog kennels, and even large goldfish bowls. There were pigeons everywhere and the sound was deafening. A couple of pigeons cooing is sweet. Three hundred is cacophony.

The visual impact was spectacular. There were fantail pigeons, Jacobin pigeons, powder pigeons, tiny Budapest tumblers, big Bokhara trumpeters, and other breeds I had rarely seen before. The visual impact had a severe downside. With so many pigeons, many of which looked alike, there was a real danger of losing track of who owned which pigeon. These buyers had paid a great deal of money for their birds, and they knew which ones were theirs because all the pigeons were banded with a numbered metal ring. Keeping track of the birds wasn't the worst complication.

All of these owners were leaving the next day to return to their respective countries, and this was February, when the weather can be problematic. Sure enough, the next day New York got hit with a giant blizzard and the airport was shut down. None of the bird owners could fly home, and so they all checked into a hotel right down the street from my store. In they came to visit their birds, and now I had to worry that one of them might try to steal some-one else's bird. It wasn't an empty concern. I could see them eye-balling one another's pigeons and whispering to one another in Arabic. Sometimes the whispering became rather loud, and I had no idea if that symbolized excitement or envy. What I didn't know was that there was a strict code of honor among these men, and I needn't have worried.

For two days, my store was like a United Nations consulate, teeming with very animated and agitated men. The craziest of all was a real wild man named Fahad. Fahad was from Kuwait, and the only one who spoke English. He was one of those people who have no fear of consequences. He traveled all over the world in search of the best pigeons, and he let nothing stand in his way. He had been making ridiculous requests since he first walked into my store. I breathed a sigh of relief when he and the others were finally able to leave, but that wasn't the last I heard from Fahad.

"Marc, this is Fahad in Kuwait. I need you to do me a favor."

What now? I thought to myself.

"Okay, Fahad, what's the matter? I'll ship the pigeons as soon as I get the permits."

"No, no, I'm not worried about the pigeons; I know you'll take care of those. I need you to call the car rental company and have them pick up the car that I rented. I had to leave it in the parking lot at the airport."

"How can you just leave it in the parking lot?" I was incredulous.

He laughed, oblivious to the presumptuousness of his request.

"It's in lot four, space twenty-two, and I left the key on top of the left front tire."

That was it. He hung up, and I dutifully called the car rental company.

"Oh, yeah, that happens all the time. It's no big deal. We just charge their credit card for the extra work to go pick the car up."

So Fahad's car got picked up, and later that week all the pigeons got shipped.

Every year, Fahad comes back to the United States for the pigeon show, and he always has me handle shipping his birds. He continues to bust my chops about everything, and I'm never surprised to get a call from Kuwait.

"Hello, Marc, this is Fahad."

"Which lot?"

CHAPTER 13

He Knows Why
the Caged Bird Sings

Pigeons in New York City may not have much stature, but in Chinatown, there is an expansive culture of singing birds. These particular birds are soft-billed and include four breeds: the hwamei, which is really a spectacled thrush; dyhal thrushes and shama thrushes; and the zosterop. The birds live in exquisitely carved cages that are specially designed so that the bird gets the maximum amount of exercise through placement of the perches. The cage builder even calculates where the bird's droppings will fall, and designs retrieval of the droppings through the bottom of the cage so as not to touch the bird's feathers or in any way "inconvenience" it. The food dishes are tiny cups made of porcelain, painted in a variety of patterns. Many of these bird owners come to me to help them design the best possible diet for their birds. The cliché from the movie *Jurassic Park,* "Spared no expense," is apt for these bird owners.

These bird owners also gather together on a regular basis to share their birds, and to see whose birds sing most beautifully. Partly, it's about competition, but mostly it's about wanting to share their special bird with other bird lovers, much like the ferret festivals in Japan. The bird owners sit around in little garden settings, drinking tea, and try to get their birds to sing the sweetest. The owner holds the tiny cage up to his face and entices the bird to perform through positive reinforcement, and he trains the bird to become a virtuoso. In truth, the bird really isn't performing for the man at all. What the Chinese know is that the bird, always a male, is ensconced in what he believes to be the most beautiful nest. His song is for the elusive female, who must approve the nest before she accepts a mate. When one male sings out that he has the best offering, another male competes with him to make his own offering. And so one bird after another competes in song for the female who isn't even there. Now, in China, these bird owners also escalate into bird fighting, again for the elusive female. In the United States, it's all about the song.

The Chinese bird owners are masters of animal husbandry. Every aspect of that bird's comfort and well-being is brought to a point of perfection.

Another area of New York City is host to a different group of people from both Trinidad and Guyana who add a Caribbean flavor to this custom. Their birds of choice are seed-eating finches, called tawa-tawa birds in their native countries. In my opinion, the tawa-tawa is the finest singing bird in the world.

Again, the cages are specially designed to provide the maximum comfort for the bird. The perches are strategically placed to keep the bird well exercised. In contrast to the Chinese cages, however, the door on these is at the bottom of the cage. The only way to open the cage is to slide the tray out, and then open the door on the bottom of the cage, thus allowing the owner to reach in and pick up the bird. That's how precious these birds are to their owners, and they take no chances that the bird might escape.

Every Sunday morning in the summer a Guyanese group meets in a park to share their birds. Each owner stakes a metal shepherd's hook into the ground and hangs the little cage from it. The cages are hung in a circle, which encourages the birds to sing in competition with one another. The winning bird is the one still singing when the others have stopped.

When I heard about this group, I decided to join the celebration to see for myself how these birds sang and competed. I went to the area I had been told about, and from the end of the park I could see the circle of birds. I walked quickly toward them, and my hurried walk toward the bird keepers probably made them fear that I was some kind of city park official, so the bird owners grabbed their cages and hooks and scattered in several directions.

Undaunted, I later contacted a friend of mine from Guyana and asked him to help me out. The next time there was a gathering, he went with me and explained who I was. It was an amazing experience. After the singing was over, I helped everybody out by clipping the birds' nails and sharing information about diet. To this day, I'm still friends with these people, and I go back to share their "circle" whenever I can.

Other parts of New York City are home to other singing bird cultures, too. Greeks and Italians have their favorite birds: goldfinches, serins, siskins, and canaries. The Italians were the first to domesticate canaries and are responsible for bringing about the beautiful color variations in the breed.

Singing birds as a culture represent the best that animal

husbandry—and pet keeping—has to offer. In order for the birds to sing, they must be happy. These birds are happy. They have the ultimate surroundings, the optimal diet, and the constant attention of a devoted human. In sharp contrast to the Maya Angelou title *I Know Why the Caged Bird Sings*, these birds are not singing as a concession to their state in life. They are celebrating life.

CHAPTER 14

Passover Pets

Some of my favorite pet keepers are Orthodox Jews, because of their attitude toward the animals in their care. While pet keeping is not formally part of their culture, my relationship with the Orthodox community is one I value highly.

These customers like and respect their pets, and they strongly believe that if you're going to have a pet, you have to treat that animal as humanely as possible. They also believe that if you can't afford to take care of that animal in the best possible way, then you really can't afford to have it at all.

Even among Orthodox Jews there are different views on pet keeping. Some think it's not appropriate for the animal to be in the house at all during the Holy Days. Others believe it's acceptable for certain "kosher" animals to live inside with the humans. I remember one woman in particular who had bought a snake for her son. Both she and her son were thrilled with his pet; and then one day, both she and her son came into my store, along with the snake.

"Mrs. R., Jason, is there something wrong with your snake?" I could see that Mrs. R. was close to tears. Jason was quiet and looked downcast.

"No, no; there's nothing wrong with the snake, but you have to take it back and find another home for it."

Jason continued to stay quiet, and it was up to me to find out what was wrong.

"So tell me, what's the problem? I mean I'm happy to find another home for the snake, but I know how much Jason liked it."

Tearfully, Mrs. R. explained that while on a visit with her rabbi, she had mentioned the snake, and he had told her that she could not keep a snake as a pet. This wasn't a matter of animals in the house during the Holy Days; this was about animals being unholy. Snakes were considered evil according to Jewish law, and she must get rid of it. Of course, I agreed to do as she asked, and then we started a conversation about what animals were considered kosher.

"Even birds can be difficult for us," she said. "I don't know all the rules, but there are three of them; and one of them says that the gizzard needs to be somehow separate from the organs around it."

I did know, from one of my other Jewish customers, that Orthodox Jews in England regarded the turkey to be a nonkosher bird, while here in the United States, turkeys were acceptable fowl. The only universal nonkosher animal is the pig.

From that same customer, who also happens to be a rabbi, I had learned that Passover was a big issue for Orthodox Jews and their pets. As many non-Jews may already know, during Passover there can be no grain products in a kosher home. This causes Orthodox pet keepers to either "lend out" their animals during this holy time, or to change the animal's diet. That's where the rabbi and I became long-term friends; and it wasn't long before he was sending members of his congregation to me in order to obtain a nongrain food that would meet kosher standards. Today, I have Orthodox Jews from all over the tristate area who come to me during Passover to buy food for their animals.

My relationship with that rabbi began with a cage full of birds nearly thirty years ago.

"Hello, Mr. Morrone; I've heard such good things about you, and I have a situation that I'm hoping you can help me with."

I didn't know that he was a rabbi, or that I was about to launch a long relationship with other Orthodox customers.

"Sure," I said, "what's the issue?"

"Well, it will soon be Passover, and I can't have certain seeds in my bird seed—no oats or corn. Can you make me a special mix that is grain-free?"

I thought for a moment and quickly realized that there were a number of seeds I could combine that would keep his house kosher.

"Not a problem. I can use millet, canary grass seed, and a couple of others. It's not an issue at all."

With that, I mixed up his specialty feed, and off he went, his birds safe for the holidays. What I didn't know was this particular rabbi was a very prominent figure in New York; and it wasn't long before I had a parade of people coming into my store asking for "kosher-for-Passover bird food." Even today, I have people coming to me from the city, Brooklyn, Burrough Park, and areas beyond those. I also create kosher foods for their rabbits, their hamsters, whatever kind of animal needs to eat grain-free food.

My Orthodox customers also love tropical fish, but even standard fish food has grain products in it, along with frozen shrimp, which are also forbidden. So I've developed a fish food made from frozen bloodworms and frozen silverside fish, both of which are acceptable to kosher standards.

Dogs are a little easier, because they are often fed from the table during Passover, which ensures that everything being fed to the dog is kosher. Dry dog food must be grain-free, and only certain brands of canned food can be fed during that time.

Mrs. R. offered another interesting piece of information related to Passover.

"You know, some of my kosher friends still won't keep their animals in the house during the Holy Days."

Actually, I already knew that from firsthand experience, but I rarely shared the information with anyone. Again, it was my same rabbi friend who needed my help with some members of his congregation who felt it would somehow "compromise" their pets to modify their diets in order to keep kosher. There were also individuals who had too many animals to keep in the house and maintain kosher standards of cleanliness. Sometimes during Passover, those families would actually leave their homes and hire a housekeeper to take care of their animals during the holy days. Others found a temporary solution for Passover, when the house has to be cleaned in a special way.

"I know some of my friends come to you with the rabbi during that time. I think that's a wonderful thing to do."

Mrs. R. was talking about the ceremony where the pet owner comes to me with an invoice signed by the rabbi, and then for one dollar I "buy" the animal and keep it in my store until the holiday is over. This exchange must be honest and pure, not at all deceptive, so the rabbi comes into my store and we participate in a blessing.

I hold the animal up in the air, and the rabbi says a special prayer over the pet and over me. The rabbi is thus endorsing that this is being done for the good of the animal, and that all parties involved are honest and pure. Fortunately, my store is large, because there are holidays where the number of animals in my care is extensive.

"Well, thank you, Mrs. R; and don't worry about the snake. I'll find him a good home."

With that, they left, and I remembered another Orthodox requirement that had been invoked only a couple of weeks earlier. This involved a couple who wanted to buy a second King Charles Spaniel, and this time they wanted a female. They had looked at me quizzically, as if I could somehow solve their dilemma.

"I'm sure I can find you a female, but you look worried."

"We don't want her to have puppies, that's the problem."

Obviously, and despite my association with the rabbi, I didn't get it.

"I can arrange to have her spayed for you. That won't be an issue."

"Oh, but that *is* the issue."

I definitely needed an explanation.

"Our rabbi says that to surgically alter an animal so it cannot reproduce is to bring bad luck into the house."

I knew that Orthodox Jews castrated sheep and cows, so I didn't understand why a dog would be so different.

"Why is it all right to surgically alter farm animals, but not a dog?"

The answer was so simple; and, again, it amplified the belief that animals should not be compromised for the benefit of the human.

"We would be spaying her for our convenience, not for her sake, and so we can't do it."

Ultimately, the couple decided to get another male dog, and the problem was resolved. This was another extension of the belief that the Orthodox pet keeper has the ultimate responsibility to take proper care of his or her animals, and to the very best of his or her ability. Kosher farm animals are raised for food, and the farmer has an obligation to maintain those animals for that purpose. If the farmer doesn't want to spend all of his time separating the males from the females, he needs to surgically alter them. The males' testosterone levels will cause them to fight with one another and adversely affect the quality of the meat. Not wanting a litter of puppies doesn't constitute a need on the part of the owner and would be considered a compromise for the dog.

My favorite Orthodox story is still the one about the famous magician, Criss Angel, and his desire to bequeath his beloved doves to a worthy child. Like me, Criss grew up on Long Island, and he and his brothers used to come into my store all the time. When he became a magician, he asked me to acquire special doves for him, and then I helped him to train them for his act. Eventually, when he left New York to go to Las Vegas, he decided to leave his little flock of doves with me. He was sad to leave them behind, but it just wasn't a practical move for the birds. Instead, he wrote a short letter and gave it to me.

> *To Whom It May Concern:*
> *My name is Criss Angel and these doves belonged to me. I hope that whoever takes these doves will work with their own magic, and love these birds as much as I have.*

So I took the doves and the letter downstairs, waiting for that right child to come into my store one day. That day occurred three months later when an Orthodox family came in with their young son, who was an aspiring magician. Skinny and tall, he reminded me of myself at his age, maybe twelve. Unlike me, he had the traditional curls and wore braces. He also impressed me as the kind of kid who got beaten up a lot, and who was ridiculed by his friends. He loved magic and performed his magic tricks at bar and bat mitzvahs, and he wanted a bird or two for his new act.

I excused myself and immediately went downstairs to retrieve the letter and the doves. I came back up with the birds and showed him the letter.

"Who's Criss Angel?"

His life was so isolated from the media that he didn't even know who Criss was. It didn't matter. I knew that this was the right child to receive the gift. He and his parents left with the doves, the letter, and a legacy of magic married to pet keeping.

PART III

ADVENTURES IN PET KEEPING

CHAPTER 15

A Typical Day in the Not-So-Typical Life of the Pet Keeper

A typical day in my life as the pet keeper starts around four in the morning, seven days a week. I don't do vacations; I don't do "date nights" with my wife; and I don't travel to exotic locations as a media person. My life totally revolves around my pet store and those media appearances that allow me to share my knowledge about animals with the world. That's my mission in life: to share my knowledge and to raise awareness for the relationship between animals and humans. My wife totally understands that. In fact, we first met when she came into my pet store looking for a job. She shares my passion and accepts the sacrifices brought about by that passion. My son, thank goodness, doesn't have that weird animal gene common to so many Morrone men. My dream for him is that he'll grow up to get a normal job with regular hours, collect a steady paycheck, and spend quality time with his own family. It's too late for me. I'm the pet keeper, and it's never going to change.

Before I walk you through my day, I want to share what it's like to run one of the largest pet stores in the world. First, there's the matter of providing the best possible food for all the animals. The produce man, Farmer Joel, comes twice a week with his big dolly full of fresh fruits and vegetables, the same organic quality that a human family would eat. Daily fresh water is a must, so we not only change the water, we also sterilize the dishes with bleach and detergent—every large or small dish. Cages have to be cleaned every day, and all the bedding replaced. We don't just have weekly garbage pickup; our garbage man comes every day. I can truly say that I have the cleanest pet store in the universe. Animal health is crucial, and I have not only one but two vets on constant call. I can imagine that some people might look at my store and think I'm rich. Or they see me on *The Martha Stewart Show* and think I must be a wealthy media personality. Truth is my passion costs money, lots of money; and every penny is worth it. Rich I'm not.

So here it is, four in the morning, and I'm out of bed in the dark. I hurtle out of my house, jump into my car, and head for Parrots of the World, which is only two minutes from my house. My sole indulgence is to stop and get a large cup of coffee and several newspapers at the local 7-Eleven. When I arrive at the store, I sit in my car for an hour and leisurely read all the newspapers while I drink my coffee. That's my luxury, my vacation. I don't want my daily "content" online. I want to feel the paper in my hands and turn real, not virtual, pages to get my fill of news. For the most part, I don't embrace technology, except as it helps to make my business easier and more efficient. I'm an old-fashioned kind of guy.

Right around five, I'm finished with my coffee and papers, and I go inside to start my business day. As soon as I walk through the door, my animals start to greet me, especially the birds. Lights go on, and the characters come to life—even the owl that has learned to become more diurnal than nocturnal because of his life with me, and the schools he visits for science days. I walk around the store, saying hello to everyone and making sure that everything's all right with the animals. Then, with a lump in my throat, I head downstairs to my office to turn on the computer and check my fax machine. Because many of my customers are on the other side of the world, bad news or problems travel at night and are there to greet me in the morning. Maybe there are orders to be filled or some problem with a shipment or some document that needs to be prepared or paperwork that needs to be redone. Whatever plans I had for the day can be quickly aborted, depending upon what's on the screen. I breathe a sigh of relief when the fax machine is empty and the Internet displays only good news.

Once I am finished with the potential nightmare in my office, I head back upstairs to what gives my life meaning. It's now around six and my employees won't arrive until around seven. I really love that hour of solitude. I start with the baby animals, checking their cages and feeding them. I love touching them, taking care of them, and seeing how much they've grown from the day before. I used to tell people that I did all of this myself because I wanted to be sure that everything was done right. The truth is I love to hold a baby macaw in my hand and watch it eat the mashed banana I put inside its beak. I love the look on the baby ferret's face when I give him fresh water. I love to get special treats like mealworms and see which finches like those. I also love to dust a handful of crickets with calcium and see which lizards are eager for them. During that one hour, I don't worry about anything. I don't think about how expensive this store is, or how many people are dependent on me for something, or how uncertain my financial future is. I am content.

So now it's seven in my store, and here comes my staff of three, all devoted to the store and me. My employees especially like the birds, and they start to feed the major ones except for my favorites, such as Harry, Remus, and Coral Ann. I also feed the animals with special needs. While my guys are cleaning cages and mopping floors, I'm back downstairs in my office to handle the onslaught of phone calls that have already started. Between calls I'm working on scripts for television, writing newspaper columns, doing paperwork, and paying bills. At ten my store opens and I'm upstairs to become the people person.

With a store like mine, I never know who's going to come through the door. What's in that big box with holes in it, being carefully carried by a scared-looking woman? Not everyone who comes in here has come in search of the perfect pet. Maybe it's a guinea pig that needs its teeth trimmed, or a bird that needs its wings trimmed, or a ferret that needs its nails trimmed. Maybe it's a litter of abandoned kittens brought in by a well-intentioned Samaritan, or a baby squirrel that's fallen out of a tree, or a pigeon hit by a car, or a box of baby raccoons left on my doorstep. One morning, I arrived to find a Great Dane tied to the parking meter in front of the store. He was obviously very ill, and ultimately I had to call Animal Control to come retrieve him. Not all deposits are cute or have happy endings. Especially in bad economic times, when people are being evicted or losing their homes to foreclosure, cherished pets from goldfish to exotic lizards find their way into my store. Even the sheriffs conducting such sad business bring me animals to place with new homes or sell. Some days I spend more time trying to place homeless animals than I do selling animals.

Between surprises, I return to my export permits and invoices, managing the machine that gives hope to all these animals.

People sometimes ask me out to lunch or to have dinner. I don't eat at all during the day. My only meal is when I finally get home, which could be ten o'clock, midnight, or any time after that. Kathi always has a good dinner for me, but she doesn't necessarily expect to share it with me. Sometimes, my days last for twenty-four hours, what with animals coming and going all day long. If a flight of pigeons arrives at JFK at three in the morning, I'm there. I can only eat when my day is over. An hour after that, it's time for bed. For me food is only f-o-o-d. It's just fuel. I don't put "food" and "pleasure" in the same sentence.

One of my genuine pleasures during the day is picking up my son after school and bringing him back to the store, where he helps me with the animal chores. He's always so cheerful about everything, and then my wife picks him up at the end of her day. We're a family who really understands one another and what our needs are. Animals aren't just in our lives; they are our lives. We all love our beautiful pet store. Everything there is the best it can possibly be. Every animal I sell is of superior quality, often bred and raised right there on the premises. The dry goods and foods I sell are the best available. We aren't just Parrots of the World; we're Pets of the World. I'm not rich, and there are days when I wonder how I can possibly compete with the chain stores and discounters who constantly threaten my existence. But I'm still here, and I'm still providing "perfect" pets in an imperfect world. I love my life as the pet keeper, a term Martha Stewart created for me. She should know. Martha is a pet keeper in her own right. I may not have a social life like most people do, but I have the life I love.

CHAPTER 16

Betta Than a Kissing Gourami

M ost people don't put "love" and "fish" in the same sentence, but I have a lifelong affection for these creatures. When I was five years old my parents got me my first fish tank for Christmas. Two weeks before that, they took me to the pet store to "look around." In the fish aisle, my mother picked up a small paperback book on tropical fish.

"Why do you want to buy that?"

"Just mind your own business. It's for me. I want to look at the pictures."

End of discussion, and I didn't think anything more about it. Christmas morning arrived, and there to my great surprise was a ten-gallon fish tank all set up in our living room. Inside the tank were two kissing gouramis, two red swordtails, two angelfish, two guppies, and a catfish. My parents had bought everything the night before, kept the fish in bags until I went to sleep, and then put it all together so it would be ready when I woke up in the morning. It was the best present I'd ever received.

That night, my little brother and my cousin took the can of fish food and dumped the whole thing into the tank. The entire tank turned milky white, and I looked sadly for any signs of my fish. Every once in a while one little fish would come close enough to the glass so that I could see it through the milky haze. Fortunately, my parents were able to completely clean the tank and save my fish.

From then on, I would watch and study them, learning everything I could by just observing. At one point, one of the guppies had babies, and I took the babies out and put them in a little jar for safekeeping. I had been told that the angelfish might eat them, and I thought it was my responsibility to protect them.

When I was eleven and we lived in Cold Spring Harbor, I dug a fishpond in the backyard and made it leakproof with a plastic liner. I filled it with goldfish and koi, and was amazed to learn how social they were. They would come to the edge when I fed them, and some would even let me touch or pet them. Even today, many people don't realize that they can "touch" animals that are accustomed to touching one another. Fish touch one another all the time; canaries don't. Odd as it sounds, you can pet your fish but not your little yellow bird. Observing my own fish, I thought of other water animals like dolphins and whales that can be trained, so I thought I might as well try to teach my fish something that would impress people who didn't think fish were smart or social.

I hung a bell with a weight attached to it by the edge of the pond, and then I dangled the weight so that it was just at the water's surface. When the fish hit the weight, I would throw in the food. Very quickly, they began hitting the weight at random times in order to get more food. Gradually, I lowered the weight deeper and deeper in the water until it was on the bottom of the pond. The fish would still hit the weight, and then I would feed them. When people came to visit, I would go over to the edge of the pond, and all the fish would go down to the bottom, hit the weight, make the bell ring, come up to the surface, and get fed. Then back down they'd go, hit the weight, make the bell ring, and back up to the surface they'd come for more food. Of course, the fish could not hear the bell; they just learned that if they hit the weight, food would come. They'd do this over and over again, just like the dolphins do at SeaWorld, and of course everyone was very impressed.

Impressing people wasn't the goal, really; I wanted to show people something they didn't already know about animals. The more knowledge we have about animals, the less likely we are to hurt them. If fish could scream and blink their eyes, maybe people wouldn't treat them so badly. If lobsters and crabs could voice their agony, maybe they wouldn't end their lives in big pots of boiling water. I like to think that I'm making fish's lives better.

Not just fish, but also other water animals that are largely misunderstood. Watching *The Undersea World of Jacques Cousteau* introduced me to the world of the octopus. Specifically, watching an octopus that had been trained to open a jar to retrieve a crab that was inside convinced me that I had to get one of those intelligent creatures. I was sixteen when I discovered that my favorite pet store had an octopus for sale. It was about the size of my fist; its mantle was about the same size. It was expensive—ninety dollars—but I had to have it. I'd been working hard and saving money since I was in elementary school, so I paid my money and bought the octopus. The clerk had one heck of a time getting the creature into a bag, and then it was back to my house where its new home would be a fifty-five-gallon saltwater fish tank. I named him Otto and in he went. By the next morning, all that was left of my resident fish were one domino damselfish and one lionfish. I had mistakenly thought that octopuses only ate crustaceans. The only reason the damselfish escaped was that she was so fast. The lionfish survived because of the poison on its dorsal fin spines. The octopus slowly stalked the lionfish, which would get down low and point all of its spines forward. Then the octopus would rush the fish, and there would be a big blast of black ink in the water. I couldn't see exactly what happened because the water was so cloudy, but at the end of it all the octopus was on one side of the tank and the lionfish was on the other.

Once I made friends with Otto, I realized how intelligent he was. Most fish do not see us as a whole person; they see us as parts—a hand with food, a finger in their mouth, a face looking at them. Otto saw the big picture. He would sit there, watching me, for hours. The fish would watch me while I fed them, and then they'd go back about their business until the next feeding. Otto watched me all the time.

If I opened the top of the tank, he would extend his tentacles up out of the tank, grab my hand, and pull it into the water. It didn't feel like he was trying to eat me; it felt more like he wanted some tactile connection to me. He would also take food from my hand. Eventually, I taught him the Jacques Cousteau trick with the glass jar. I would hold the jar just out of the water, and he would un-screw the lid, remove the crab, and go back into the water to eat it. That lid wasn't loosely screwed, either. I had started out with a loosely screwed lid, but I continued tightening it until it would have been difficult for a human to open. He never learned to screw the lid back on, though.

Otto lived with me for almost a year, a long time for an octopus. I've had many more over the years, and I do sell them in my pet store. I also sell lionfish, carefully.

One day back in the 1980s, one of my employees got stung

while cleaning the tank with lionfish in it. It was only a little prick on one finger, but I wasn't going to take any chances, and I drove him to the emergency room. The ER doctor looked at the finger and told me what I had expected to hear.

"Well, it's only a fish sting. Go get some meat tenderizer and that will help. The active ingredient in tenderizer is papain, which will break down the poison."

Across the street from my old store was a Greek diner owned by my good friend George. He had a very thick accent, and he didn't always understand me so well.

"George, I need some meat tenderizer to use on this kid's hand. He's got poison from a fish sting, and the doctor said to get some tenderizer."

"Ah, you need meat tenderizer. Okay, I go get it."

He went downstairs and came back up with a big wooden mallet.

"Okay, you hold hand down and I pound it. I pound out the poison."

Trying not to laugh, I tried to explain. Not well enough.

"Okay, what you want do, you want to hold hand down and I hit the hand with the meat tenderizer, and that drain out the poison? I never heard that, but I do it if you say."

I thanked him for trying to help, went to the supermarket, and put Adolph's meat tenderizer on the wound instead. Lionfish are beautiful to look at, but not delightful to hold.

Much sweeter and almost otherworldly are sea horses, and I started buying those while I was still in high school. For six dollars, I received from Florida a little plastic cubicle containing a package of sea salt, a pack of brine shrimp eggs, and a little bag with two sea horses in it. For an extra dollar, I could get three more sea horses, including a pregnant male who could have as many as twenty babies. I'd put them in fish bowls, following all the instructions in the package, but they rarely lived more than a week. Today, aquarium pet keeping has reached a level where sea horses can be kept for years. They don't need brine shrimp eggs, and they can thrive on frozen shrimp or even fish flakes.

Forty years ago, fish were treated as nearly worthless commodities. Today, fish have acquired a kind of special status. They're bred domestically, not imported. They're no longer wild fish kept captive. For those who object to fish living in "glass boxes," it's important to remember that even in the wild the majority of fish live in their own prescribed domain. The movie *Finding Nemo* was a very accurate view of the world through a fish's eye. Pelagic fish like tuna and bluefish are different, traveling a wide domain. Pelagic fish are rarely in the same place twice. Mackerel, although not a big fish like tuna or bluefish, is also a pelagic fish.

Today, there are also breed standards for fish, just like there are for dogs. The best fish must conform to that particular breed's template. There are even fish shows and hobbyist groups. In Japan, the koi is king. In China, it's the goldfish. In this country, the most popular breeds tend to be bettas, the Siamese fighting fish, which originated in Southeast Asia and which can live comfortably in small bowls without filtration, just routinely cleaned water. Other breeds include goldfish, tetras, danios, and barbs. A new type of fish that has become especially popular is the African cichlid. There are many different types and colors, but they tend to be aggressive toward one another. African cichlids and certain other species originated in the Rift Lakes of Africa, where minerals literally from the center of the earth have leached into the waters, making the water hard and alkaline. As a result, cichlids have thrived and evolved to partake of many different food sources in these lakes. Some eat at the surface, some live in the shoals, some graze, and some eat at a deeper level in the water. In contrast, a North American lake might have bass and pickerel that eat other fish, sucker fish that graze, and sunfish that eat insects. Those are all different kinds of fish. In the African lake, they're all cichlids, which evolved to eat the different foods available.

Some of these cichlids are mouth brooders, which means the mother keeps the babies in her mouth. With other cichlids, there is an actual nest where the mother lays the eggs and both parents watch over them. When the babies start to hatch, the parents pick them up and carry them back to the nest until they're mature enough to survive on their own.

On one occasion while I was raising cichlids, I observed the father gathering his babies. A piece of food fell in front of him, just after he had picked up one of the babies in his mouth. With the baby in his mouth, he grabbed the food and stood absolutely still for at least twenty seconds. All of a sudden, he spat out the food and the baby, ate the food, and picked up the baby again. He went back to the nest and deposited his offspring. I asked myself, "Is that an instinctive act or a cognitive one?" A scientist would likely opt for the former, but I had to wonder. Why had the fish stopped for those twenty seconds? Was it "thinking" about what to do next?

That incident reminded me of my childhood when I was seven or eight. I had a tank with two kissing gouramis, two swordtails, one angelfish, two guppies, and one catfish. The swordtails and guppies were livebearers, and it wasn't long before I had baby fish. My book about caring for fish said that the angelfish would eat the babies, so I had to find a way to save them. I took the plastic army helmet someone had given me—someone who didn't realize that I made baby fish, not war—and filled it with water. I put the baby fish inside and to my delight they thrived. When they were mature enough, I took them out of their "nest" and put them back in the tank with the big fish.

Today, at home, I have a 125-gallon tank with lots of community fish: mollies, swordtails, and danios. I also have a pond with numerous goldfish. My wife likes bettas, and she has several of those.

My life has been one continuing stream of animals, not all of which have fur or feathers.

The "Great Mother"
of All Hamsters

Small and furry, hamsters are a familiar and longstanding part of the American pet scene. Konrad Lorenz, best known for his work with birds, had a particular passion for the hamsters he kept in a vivarium on his desk.

I read about his hamsters when I was very young, maybe ten years old, and it started a lifelong interest in these frequently trivialized animals.

Fact: all the hamsters kept as pets throughout the entire world are descendants of only three hamsters in the Syrian Desert.

In the 1930s, a scientist was traveling in the Sinai Peninsula when he discovered a hole in the ground. The hole intrigued him, and he dug it out, discovering a female golden hamster—the Great Mother of all the hamsters that we keep as pets today—with her babies. The number of babies may be disputed, but not the Great Mother. In any case, the scientist took the hamsters back to the University of Jerusalem, where most of the babies died, but three adults survived. The baby wheel started, and from there, selective breeding brought about a proliferation of variety in colors and fur patterns, from hairless to long, flowing hair—the ones we call Teddy Bear hamsters.

Hamsters even have categories: polar bear teddies, black bear hamsters, ivory hamsters, and, of course, hairless hamsters. At the core, they're all golden hamsters. There's not a toothless, banjo-playing rodent among them. Apparently, inbreeding isn't a problem for hamsters.

More good news for hamsters, gerbils, degus, guinea pigs, rats, mice, and dwarf hamsters is that the surplus of rodents being used in laboratories has spilled over into the pet market. The degu, which looks more like a gerbil but is really more like a chinchilla, was originally imported from Chile to be used in diabetes studies. Degus are prone to contract diabetes, and this made them ideal for such studies. No one seems to know who figured out that degus could be diabetic. Perhaps someone reading this book will be able to enlighten me. What we do know is that if degus eat too much fruit, they develop too much sugar in their systems, and thus become diabetics. People who keep degus as pets need to remember that.

The "pocket pets" we see in pet stores are all domesticated. The breeders may not be deliberately changing the way the animal looks, but they're definitely changing the way the animal acts. Rodents who bite when you pick them up are selectively bred out as not being suitable to live with humans. That's why rodents are so well suited for children, especially.

Once the rodent has been bred for gentleness, and is no longer living in fear, serotonin levels drop to zero. Now, other spontaneous mutations can occur, like unusual colors and hair variations, because the drop in serotonin allows these mutations to occur. Again, no one quite knows why that's true, but the results speak for themselves.

The chinchilla is a good example of a mutation that cuts both ways. In the wild, it was hunted almost into extinction for its softer-than-soft coat. Once captured and domesticated by people more interested in the animal for itself, many changes occurred. The chinchilla of the 1920s, indeed of the 1950s, when many American households raised chinchillas as moneymakers, is very different from the chinchilla today. Contemporary chinchillas come in many different colors beyond the standard gray, and they are much more docile and friendly. Even better for today's chinchillas is that no one wears chinchilla coats anymore, so breeders have turned their attention to the pet market. Martha Stewart keeps chinchillas and knows firsthand what delightful pets they make. They don't have claws, because in their natural state they jump all over rocks. Their claws disappeared; instead, they have tiny, stubby fingers similar to the hooves of a mountain goat. Their soft, velvety hair, which got them into trouble in the first place, requires dust to help remove the dirt. Rolling in dust and giving themselves a good shake helps to rid them of deeper dirt and thus ensure that soft, velvety coat.

The evolution of chinchillas is similar to that for foxes bred for their pelts. The tamer the fox, the more variety in its appearance. New colors appeared, ears flopped, tails curled. The snarling, aggressive fox of one generation eventually became the docile, more colorful fox of generations down the line.

That said, few people are going to consider a fox for a pet, but the visual similarities to foxes is interesting.

The pocket pet, which includes the often misunderstood mouse and rat, makes a wonderful pet for all ages. They can respond to their name, they're totally sentient, they're aware of themselves, and they're aware of humans. They're also clean and easy to maintain.

Ideally, the child with a pocket pet no longer sees it as "something he has to take care of," but as a sentient animal. The child feeds "Hammy" because "Hammy" is an individual who needs to eat. The child cleans "Hammy's" cage because "Hammy" deserves to live in a clean cage. The child takes care of "Hammy" not because he's forced to, but because he understands the rights and needs of his pocket pet. Caring for pocket pets is really a simple affair. As long as the water bottle has fresh water in it, the food is fresh every day, and the cage is cleaned once a week, the upkeep on one of these pocket pets is not difficult or time-consuming.

Too many well-meaning parents get a pet for their child in order to teach him or her a sense of responsibility. Nothing could be further from reality. Taking out the garbage teaches a child responsibility. Taking care of a hamster or other pocket pet shouldn't be a chore. Taking care of that pet should be something the child does because he or she feels compassion for the animal. A creature with two eyes, a nose, two ears, and a cute little round face can inspire that compassion.

There are of course differences among all of these pocket pets.

Hamsters are solitary animals; they like to stay by themselves. They're also nocturnal and prefer to sleep during the day. If a child wakes up a hamster at three in the afternoon, it's likely to be cranky and won't want to play. In addition, two hamsters in one cage can lead to fights between the two. Gerbils, on the other hand, are social, so you can keep two male gerbils if they're brothers, or two female gerbils if they're sisters, together in the same cage and they'll be fine. They're also diurnal, which means they're awake all day and ready to play when the child is.

Rats and mice also make wonderful pets; they just have bad press agents. Too many people hear "rat" and think "plague." Others hear "mouse" and think house infestation. The rats and mice bred to be pets are just that, pets. They're not dirty and they don't carry disease. Pet owners have a better chance of getting sick from their dog or cat.

By contrast, in Japan rodents are regarded as the ideal child's pet, along with hamsters, gerbils, mice, chinchillas, hedgehogs, flying squirrels, and chipmunks. None of these are treated as a child's pet; they're treated as a serious pet, and are kept with all the best tenets of good animal husbandry.

When I'm appearing in a television segment where I'm featuring hamsters, gerbils, degus, or whatever rodents they might happen to be, I always go out of my way to promote how fascinating these animals are. I also point out that hamsters captivated one of the most famous animal experts in the world. I know in my heart that there are countless kids out there who for whatever reason can't have a cat or dog, and that their only pet option is one of these rodents. The pet-loving child is somehow diminished by his or her lack of ability to have one of the socially "approved" pets, the dog or the cat. I've seen children teased because they "only" had a hamster or a gerbil or a rat. I want those children to feel proud of their animals, and not feel that they're second-class pet owners. Maybe they'll even look at a map to find out where Mongolia is because their gerbil originated from there. Maybe they'll get a book about Syria to find out more about their hamster's original home.

In the United States, largely because they're small and more easily disposable, we think of pocket pets as disposable commodities. A couple of months ago, a woman came into my store with a guinea pig in a cage.

"You have to take this guinea pig."

The woman was very well dressed, tanned, and fit. She was not someone down on her luck who needed me to find a home for the animal she could no longer afford to take care of.

"You have to take this guinea pig off my hands. I can't keep it anymore."

She plunked it down on the counter as if she were returning an unsatisfactory pair of shoes to Bloomingdale's.

"Just what's the problem? Why can't you keep the guinea pig?"

I already knew that I would gladly take her pet, but I just needed to ask. Suddenly, I felt a little like the bemused clerk at Bloomingdale's.

She put both her hands on the counter, squinted her eyes, and hissed at me.

"This animal's mere existence is an inconvenience to my lifestyle."

If the guinea pig had been shoes, I would have thrown them at her. I'll never forget those words. I'll never forget the way she slanted her eyes and hissed those words at me.

That's one of the big reasons I go on television and talk about all pets, not just cats and dogs, or even birds. I want children who hear about hamsters or gerbils or any of those pocket pets to feel proud of their pet, and not feel as if they have to apologize for not having a "better" pet. I want children, and adults, to look at their hamsters and think to themselves what great pets they are, and realize that pocket pets are not disposable. I want them to be more like the Japanese, who are openly proud of their hamsters, no explanations or apologies offered.

CHAPTER 18

A Giant Rabbit Called Harvey

Another American favorite are rabbits. What fascinated me about rabbits from a very young age were the colors. My friend Michael, who lived around the corner from me during elementary school, had two Dutch rabbits, a brown and white male and a black and white female. When the rabbits had babies, I was intrigued by the color variations and curious why they occurred. It wasn't until sixth grade that our science teacher taught us about genetics, a subject that still intrigues me as an adult.

I started keeping rabbits around that time, and they all lived in hutches out in the backyard. I'd watch them for hours, and it always seemed as if they were hiding something from me. Much later, when I was sixteen and read *Watership Down,* I finally realized what it was they were hiding.

Fear. In the wild, rabbits live in a constant state of fear because of all the predators wanting to kill them. Outside in their hutches, my rabbits never felt safe. At night, raccoons must have approached their hutches, trying to break in. The rabbits had no way of knowing that their hutches were secure. So, my rabbits never let down their guard, and I was never able to feel close to them.

Watership Down, by Richard Adams, is one of those "three books I would take to a desert island" choices. The other two would be

The Yearling, by Marjorie Kinnan Rawlings, and *The Godfather*, by Mario Puzo. Of the thousands of books in my house, those three are the big winners.

Adams based his book on a study of rabbits called *The Private Life of the Rabbit*. After reading Adams's book, I read the one on which he based *Watership Down*. Between the two books, I completely understood about rabbits' social structure, what rabbits do, and how they think. As a character, I decided that I was Hazel, the rabbit who does all the thinking and takes all the chances.

In the case of my rabbits, what would Hazel do?

I moved all of my rabbits indoors, and the transformation was nothing less than amazing. Their personalities blossomed; they danced, literally; they played; and they would interact with me. Ever since that teen revelation, I've kept rabbits as house pets, not caged animals. Many years later, a group called the House Rabbit Society was formed, and its mission was to promote rabbits as house pets. I had been doing that for several years beforehand. Even today, everything I say about rabbits on television is in accord with that organization.

Of all the rabbits I've had or still have, my favorite rabbit is Harvey, a giant Flemish rabbit. He appears with me all the time on television, and is a star in his own right. He came to me in a rather odd way.

One day I got a call from the police out in Shoreham, a town on Long Island. A couple that lived there had seen this giant rabbit in their backyard, and they were concerned. At the time, there was talk of putting a nuclear reactor out there, and the townspeople were more than a little spooked. The woman who called the police was afraid that there was already nuclear presence, and that it was leaching into the water supply, thus producing giant creatures. The police went to her house, retrieved Harvey, and promptly gave me a call. They said he had a tattoo in his ear, which meant he had been a show rabbit. They brought him over to me, and he's been with me ever since.

He quickly became one of the star animals in my menagerie because he's so big. He's also incredibly easygoing. I can take him anywhere and he gets along with everyone. I just plunk him down with dogs, cats, monkeys, whatever, and he just sits there and stares, with this droll expression on his face. He also has a secret. What he doesn't know is that I know what it is. He is cynical about the rest of the world, and he never lets his guard down. He's always holding back something—just in case. Ironically, and despite his view of the world, he's probably been on television more than any other rabbit in the history of the world. He's very, very dear to me, as are all of my rabbits. When someone drops off a rabbit in a box outside my door, I am mystified as to how someone could do that.

Sometimes, the person dropping off a rabbit comes right into the store with it. That happened a few months ago. This woman walked into the store with a rabbit in a cage, and literally slammed the cage down on the counter.

"You've got to take this rabbit off my hands."

Shades of the guinea pig woman came to mind. This woman was also well dressed, fit, and enhanced by cosmetic surgery. She was older than the other woman, but very pretty. If I'd passed her on the street, I'd have probably thought to myself, *She seems like a nice person.*

"Okay, ma'am, I'll find a home for him."

But I just couldn't leave well enough alone.

"Out of curiosity, what does this bunny do that makes you not like it so much?"

Uh-oh. Palms on the counter and eyes slanted, she made her position clear.

"He's an inconvenience to my lifestyle."

Were those two women related? Maybe the women had heard someone say that, and thought it was pithy. In any case, I did appreciate her brutal honesty, and off she went without her inconvenient rabbit.

(Speaking of brutal honesty, I must return to Harvey for a moment. Technically speaking, there are two Harveys. The first Harvey lived for ten years after I got him. The Harvey people see on television today, or in my shop, is the second Harvey, and he's nine years old.)

Rabbits can make great and convenient pets, but the only way to have an optimal relationship with one rabbit is to make sure that he feels safe. Inconsistent treatment or threatening behavior will cause the rabbit to revert to its fear standard, and it will live out its life on guard.

One of my friends, a woman named Carol, had a Dutch Miniature that lived freely in her house, was box-trained, and was extraordinarily affectionate with her. Carol was married, but divorce was in the cards. During the last few months before they were divorced, there was considerable tension and many loud exchanges between Carol and her husband. After Carol was out on her own, her rabbit behaved differently. He was jumpy and distant. He never recovered from the sense of fear that had developed during that breakup. Carol said the worst thing about the divorce was the loss of her relationship with that rabbit.

In the world of rabbit marriage, the buck is very loyal to his doe. In domesticated groups, all the rabbits work together. The North American cottontail, in contrast, is a solitary creature that doesn't socialize at all, and it will fight with other rabbits that encroach on its territory or threaten its food. Even if someone captured a baby cottontail and raised it with great affection, the adult rabbit would still see its owner as a cottontail and fight with it. The rabbits in *Watership Down* are accurate representations of rabbits that live in groups. Each rabbit character has a particular talent that is unique to it, and to rabbits in the wild. One rabbit is a very good fighter, another is a very good runner, another can figure his way out of traps, another is a great leader, and yet another has a heightened sensitivity for danger. Most movies in which animals talk are pure fantasy. In Adams's novel, the rabbits talk about rabbit things: mating, grass, getting away from foxes.

The rabbits we keep as pets are descendants of those wild European rabbits depicted in *Watership Down*. They share the same kinds of sensibilities expressed by those characters. As pets owners, we can at least minimize some of their instinctual fears. First of all, we can neuter them so that hormones don't make them combative. In the wild, rabbits can get away from a rabbit with raging hormones. That's not so easy in your home. Secondly, we don't need to be concerned that having two rabbits will prevent us from having a relationship with our pets. As I've learned from my long experience with rabbits, the more the merrier. Next, be kind to your rabbits. Don't make them somehow fear for their lives. Finally, and most important, people who choose rabbits as pets should remember that we share one very important characteristic with them. Both humans and rabbits share the will to endure, no matter what the adversity might be. From my perspective, this is truer in our relationships with rabbits than with other animals. A fox might be chasing a rabbit, and the rabbit is running this way and that, terrified that at any moment the fox will snatch it. Humans must contend with human foxes that threaten us in different ways. When the rabbit finally escapes from the fox, it stops and looks around. If nothing is there to bother it, the rabbit just starts eating grass and goes on with its life. Rabbits understand "just letting it be."

CHAPTER 19

Puff, the Magic Iguana

At the opposite end of the spectrum from "warm and furry" is "cold and slithery." Reptiles are fairly new to the pet-keeping scene. Thirty or forty years ago, most of the reptiles making their way into American households were little green anoles, better known back then as chameleons. I remember getting one of those at a carnival. The poor little creature was tied to a tiny, light chain that clipped onto a person's collar or lapel. The man who sold it to my parents told us exactly how to take care of it.

"Yeah, you just feed it sugar water and it'll be fine."

Like most of its fellow anoles sold at such places, it died within a few days. Everyone thought of them as disposable. When I was older, I learned that not only were they not called chameleons, but their care was much more complicated than what we had been told years earlier. Anoles are only called chameleons because of their ability to change colors. In order for anoles to thrive, their environments must be managed carefully.

First of all, anoles cannot live on sugar water. In fact, they can't even drink water out of a dish. In order to stay hydrated, they have to be misted with warm water from a plant mister every day. They eat crickets dusted with a special vitamin powder. Within their habitat, both the temperature and humidity have to be carefully maintained. All of this is a far cry from pinning one to your shirt and feeding it sucrose.

Little baby turtles have often shared the same fate as anoles. More than once when I was a child, my father would bring home two baby turtles in a little plastic bowl with a little island in the middle. The little island had a tiny plastic palm tree, and the whole setup included a small jar of something called "turtle food," which was actually no more than dried fly larvae. Everyone was so surprised when the turtles died. I couldn't figure out what I was doing wrong, and so my father would bring home another turtle "habitat," and the sad cycle would repeat itself.

What no one understood is similar to the original plight of anoles. First of all, turtles require fresh water. The water in those early turtle bowls got changed maybe once a week, if that. The bowl became a veritable sewer of bacteria, especially salmonella, which children would contract after sticking their fingers into the turtle's bowl. Turtles also require temperatures of 80 to 85 degrees in order to survive. Sitting there on the dining room table at room temperature was a sure way to guarantee that that didn't happen. Their diet needed to be much more than dried flies that have absolutely no calcium in them. A turtle's shell is made of calcium, and turtles need a high-protein, high-calcium diet. After thousands and thousands of turtle deaths, along with a high number of salmonella infections in humans, the government made the sale of baby turtles illegal. They're still illegal today.

Turtles got the last laugh on that one.

Other reptiles—iguanas and snakes—that had been imported for the pet trade also died in huge numbers because of the parasites with which they were infested. Back during my childhood years, the only zoo that really understood reptiles was the Staten Island Zoo. They understood parasite control and proper diet, so their reptile collection was for a long time one of the best in the world.

Over the past thirty years, reptile husbandry has become as intense as dog and cat husbandry. The reptiles kept today as pets have all been born in captivity and are practically domesticated. The bearded dragons, leopard geckos, and ball pythons that we keep and breed look and act totally different from their wild counterparts. These reptiles live long, healthy lives and are responsive to the humans who keep them. Those poor reptiles we kept prior to that were literally dying when we got them. They were dying the entire time we had them as pets, some taking months to die. Since the reptile had no way of expressing itself, we had no way of knowing the measure of its suffering. And because of all that suffering and premature death, we were never able to know their personalities.

Today, the healthy reptiles we keep as pets demonstrate a great deal of personality. They're also totally sentient, and they recognize both themselves and humans as individuals. For those children or adults with allergies, reptiles are perfect pets.

We've even learned how to gauge the "emotions" of reptiles. Certain reptiles have certain ways of communicating with one another. For instance, when a male bearded dragon sees another male bearded dragon, as a greeting it will bob its head up and down and flare out its throat. Then the throat will turn black. A female bearded dragon will bow her head up and down, and then lift up her front leg and wave it around in a circular motion. Once the lizard recognizes that we're not going to hurt it, it will acknowledge humans in the same way. Iguanas will communicate with us in the same way as the bearded dragon.

When it comes to "emotions," the iguana is an excellent example.

Before I was married, I lived alone in a studio apartment. One day, someone dropped off a very large, six-foot-long iguana on my doorstep at Parrots of the World. I named him Puff, and I had a problem. He was too large to keep in the store, so I took him home and set him up in a large glass aquarium. He promptly broke out of the aquarium and made himself comfortable in the kitchen sink. He also defecated in the sink.

Mmm, what to make of that?

Back in his cage, he wouldn't go to the bathroom at all.

Gee, it's almost like . . . No, that can't be true. He doesn't want to go to the bathroom in his cage?

Exactly, just like a dog. I decided to put up a shelf over the kitchen sink and under the window to see what would happen. I also carpeted the shelf and installed a heat lamp over it. Sure enough, he broke out of his cage and set up residence on the shelf. Cleaning up after him was easy.

He'd stay there all during the day. When I came home at night, I would cut up fruits and vegetables for his dinner, put it in the sink, and turn on the faucet. He would crawl off the shelf, get onto the kitchen counter, crawl into the sink, eat, and drink water from the running faucet. After that he would make a large doody in the sink, and I would simply flush it down the drain. Back up onto his shelf he'd go, and both of us were happy.

After a while, he expanded his culinary taste. On very late nights at the store, I would pick up Chinese food, take it home, and sit down on the sofa to eat it. I saw Puff watching me, and one night he climbed down off his shelf onto the counter, jumped onto the floor, crawled all the way over to where I was sitting, climbed up on the couch and slid onto my lap, where he sampled whatever I was eating. Then back to the sink he went. No muss, no fuss.

In places like Aruba, where people vacation, and in Florida, where feral iguanas are numerous, iguanas insinuate themselves into our activities. In Aruba, iguanas will climb right up onto the tourists' laps and beg for food. In Florida, feral iguanas will raid barbecues and backyard parties. My iguana, because he was healthy and felt safe, also felt free to interact with me, just as he might with other iguanas. So there I was in my studio apartment, enjoying my relationship with a house-trained reptile.

Today, iguanas are also unique because they are farmed. They're farmed partly because people like to eat them. I first learned about this from my friend Tony, who's from El Salvador. I used to get my baby iguanas from him, which I later exported to other parts of the world or sold in my store. Being the curious person I am, I wanted to know how they farmed iguanas, and Tony gave me the big picture.

The farmers fence in an area about the size of a football field with corrugated metal sheets about six feet high. Over the top of the enclosure is a net that keeps the iguanas in and the predatory birds and other animals out. Baby iguanas are especially vulnerable to predators because they're only six inches long. Almost anything can eat them.

Next to the iguana pens is the truck farm, where the farmers raise cucumbers and other vegetables to feed the iguanas. As the vegetables grow, the farmers just throw the food over the fence into the iguana pens. The iguanas produced in those pens are not domesticated, just kept. The farmers are not selectively breeding them, just keeping and raising them. When the females start building their nests, the farmers find ways to attract them to the softer sand. When the iguanas lay their eggs, the farmers go inside the pens, dig them up, and transfer them to the nursery, where they're raised in incubators. The farmers do that because it would be very difficult to catch the baby iguanas loose in the pens.

When the babies hatch, they are all given CITES permits so that they can be exported. The Salvadoran government also watchdogs the operation to make sure that the farmers don't supplement their egg supply with wild iguana eggs from out in the forest. The government periodically visits the pens, does a count of the males and females, and makes an approximation of how many eggs should be produced from those iguanas. It's not an exact science, but it helps control wild versus captive animals.

The baby iguanas, once permitted, are on their way to countries all over the world, including the United States. Not all of the baby iguanas are exported; some are put back in the pens where they grow up to become . . .

Food.

I could hardly believe the first time Tony showed me cans and cans of iguana soup, and packages of frozen iguana meat. All of these items were being sold in delicatessens in Salvadoran neighborhoods in New York City. Even those items had to be certified by CITES. The value of iguanas as food is very high and extends all throughout Central America. I've personally never tasted iguana meat, and it's not likely I ever will. I would imagine, since it's reptilian, that it tastes like a cross between chicken and bluefish. I prefer my iguanas on the claw.

I still get all of my iguanas from El Salvador, as do other retailers and the like. It's far cheaper—five to seven dollars each—to get them from those iguana farmers. That cheap cost does lead to some abuses. Long after chameleons disappeared from the carnival scene, baby iguanas can still be found being offered as prizes at carnivals and Renaissance fairs. At the latter, they're given exotic names like St. George's Dragons. Despite the name, their fate is much like that of the early anoles. Most of them die because a baby iguana requires more care than a puppy does. The ones who survive develop into six-foot-long, ten-pound lizards that have an excellent chance of ending up in a box on my doorstep.

Perhaps my biggest contribution to keeping pet iguanas, aside from rescuing those abandoned at my store, was resolving their water issue. The original inspiration for my creation came from Puff, back in my studio apartment days. I'd watch him drinking from the running faucet, and thought to myself, *I wonder if he would drink from a water bottle, like hamsters, monkeys, dogs, and so many other animals?* From a practical standpoint, keeping the typical iguana's cage water clean was a nightmare, because the iguana would drop food into it and generally foul the water in a very short period of time.

I chose a water bottle used for hamsters, and painted the tip red. I figured that iguanas, being the curious creatures they are, would bite at the tip, and "Eureka!" Sure enough, Puff converted to the water bottle. I was proud of myself for solving the water issue for iguanas.

This all happened in the early days of the Internet. I had just done a segment on using water bottles to feed iguanas, and I naively expected iguana owners to applaud me for my discovery.

How wrong I was. Letters poured in, angry letters asserting that the old way was best. Beyond the letters, I was flamed on the Internet, and I felt devastated. Today, I get flamed all the time, and it doesn't bother me at all. But back then it was a cruel slap for having found a way to make iguanas happier and healthier.

It was a good time to remember the words I would later learn from Martha Stewart: "You can't please everyone, so just focus on the ones you do." Puff concurs.

CHAPTER 20

For Emily, Wherever I Hope to Find Her

guanas tend to be more socially interactive than some other reptiles. Back in the seventies and eighties, virtually any breed could
be imported, bred, and sold, and there were no restrictions on what
kinds of reptiles could be sold as pets. This included huge boa constrictors and highly poisonous snakes, but certainly the most popular were the large constricting snakes, including Burmese pythons.

Ball pythons, imported from West Africa, were and still are a
favorite snake choice. This species is an excellent example of how
an indigenous people can be "incentive encouraged" to help
preserve their environment and its endangered species. During
the python's breeding season, the people go out and catch adult
female pythons that are gravid, or full of eggs. They take the snakes
back to the coast or their village, and keep them in enclosures until
the animals lay their eggs. Once the eggs are laid, they are gathered up, incubated, and hatched, and the baby snakes are exported
all over the world. The mother snakes are returned to the wild,
where they continue to breed, and the cycle is repeated. Before
there was a commercial interest in these animals, the natives

killed and ate them, threatening future populations. These same natives are now learning more about these reptiles to maximize breeding potential. They have become environmentalists without realizing it.

The snakes conceived in the wild but raised in captivity are still wild animals—not dangerous, just wild. Certain snake hobbyists raise ball pythons in captivity, but they selectively breed for different colors. The selectively bred snakes can be white, yellow, black, brown, or any combination. Where pythons from West Africa will sell here in the United States for about fifty dollars, specially bred snakes can sell anywhere from three hundred to three thousand dollars.

As pets, whether at the high or low end of the cost scale, ball pythons are very gentle and never get larger than four feet in length. They're perfect for a child, or for anyone who might want to impress their friends with owning a snake. I was literally "impressed" with one of the ball python's larger relatives, the Burmese python.

Emily, as I named her, was my favorite snake and appeared with me both on television and in print ads because she was so friendly and easy to work with. Burmese pythons are beautifully marked, and I'm sure her presence in the media helped to influence new buyers who imagined that all pythons were just as friendly and easy to be around.

Every night before I left the store, I would put Emily back in her cage, a ritual she accepted without protest. There she would stay until the next day's media activities; or if none were scheduled, she would lounge comfortably in her cage. A "media darling," she had come to enjoy the adulation of people around her, so visitors to the store seemed to please her. She was my best reptile representative.

One particular morning I arrived well before five a.m. I was as usual the first in the store. Most of my employees wouldn't arrive for an hour or so, and my early appearance gave me a chance to make sure everything was in order before anyone else showed up.

"Hi, Harry. Hi, Remus. Hello, guys. Hello, Emily."

"Emily? Hello, Emily?" No Emily. Her cage was open and she was nowhere in sight. I stopped and looked around. A sixteen-foot snake can't hide that easily.

"Oh, my god. No, Emily, no!"

She had managed to break into the enclosure where the baby rabbits were and had one of them in her mouth. Unlike most breeders and pet owners, I didn't feed my snakes live mice, so the sight of Emily with a live rabbit in her jaws horrified me.

"No, Emily, no!" I knew my words were useless as I watched her slowly squeezing the life out of the little bunny.

Because she was so tame, I was able to grab her, struggling to get the rabbit out of her mouth. I stood there, holding her head at arm's length, while the rest of her body stretched down to the floor and lay uncoiled for another ten feet. The teeth of a python curve backward, so I actually had to first push the rabbit farther down into her throat, allowing the teeth to exit the flesh; then I quickly snatched the still-live bunny out. Emily was no longer a friendly snake; she was enraged that I was trying to steal her prey. I should say that I believed she was enraged, because she immediately tried to snatch back the rabbit. She missed, and now my entire wrist was stuck in her mouth. I had become the rabbit replacement.

I found myself completely encased in Emily's coils; only my head and part of my left hand weren't in her grasp.

"Okay," I said to myself. "How am I going to get out of this one?"

Right about that time, three of my employees came in. All three come from the Dominican Republic, where every snake is considered dangerous. Because you can't tell which snakes are poisonous and which aren't, you live a lot longer if you just avoid all snakes. In the sugarcane fields, there's just not enough time to determine if the snake wriggling in the underbrush is a highly poisonous fer-de-lance or a harmless rat snake.

"Hey, guys, can you give me a hand?"

All three bolted for the door, nearly tripping over one another. They looked like characters in a Bugs Bunny cartoon, scrambling to escape. I wasn't really surprised, or even angry for that matter. They'd seen me get out of many serious scrapes, and they considered me somewhat invincible. And after all, this was a snake.

"Okay, so I guess I'm all alone."

My first and best thought was to somehow get her head under hot water. Snakes hate hot water. It wouldn't scald her, just make her jaws relax so I could escape. I had to get her to a water source, a tricky business because I was still wrapped in her coils. By now my hand was dripping blood, and I needed to move fast.

Moving fast wasn't really an option, but at least I had a plan. The utility sink was only about ten feet away. That would work. Waddling like a penguin, I painfully made my way to the sink, inching my way across the floor, weighted down by a 150-pound python. Finally I reached the faucet, and with my free left hand managed to turn on the hot water. Now came the most challenging part. I had to rotate my body so that my right hand—which was fully in her mouth—could be placed under the hot water.

Eventually it worked. The hot water caused her to relax her constricting coils, and I was able to retrieve my other hand and unwrap myself. I then lifted her back into her cage, and began to nurse my mangled hand. I quickly called one of the vets on call, and he came right over. He bandaged my hand and that was that. My hand healed without permanent damage and Emily seemed to accept without malice her life in confinement.

What the experience impressed upon me was my opposition to feeding live animals to snakes. Back in the seventies and eighties, and even today, pet owners liked to feed their snakes live mice. Part of me says, "Sure, go ahead; watch that snake eating a live mouse. Maybe that will help reduce your aggressions and you won't rob my car or my house, or beat me up." But most of me says no.

Feeding live animals to reptiles is the totally wrong thing to do. In the wild, snakes are ambush predators. They don't seek out another animal to eat; they lie in wait, hiding, until a suitable prey animal walks past. Then they reach out and grab it from behind. They're all about the ambush.

If you put a mouse or a rat in a cage with the snake, the rodent has the distinct advantage—at least for a while—and the rodent will try to bite the snake. Snakes have very soft and delicate skin, and the sepsis from the bite has the potential to kill the snake.

So when I saw domestically owned snakes being fed live rodents, I decided there had to be a better way. Why did these snakes have to eat live animals? Nobody would believe me, but I began to experiment. I knew that poisonous snakes such as rattlesnakes wanted to subdue their prey without getting hurt. So a quick kill means the snake can leave the victim to die ten feet away, and then eat at its own leisure. My idea to feed dead animals to snakes came from that behavior.

First, I tried using dead mice and rats, and sure enough, the snakes ate them as readily. After that, I was able to teach my snakes to eat chicken legs and thighs. I simply tied a chicken leg to the dead rat; the snake would first eat the chicken, then the rat. Then I graduated to using thawed out chicken parts so I could keep them frozen.

"Wow, this really works."

Of course, no one in the seventies believed me. Today, there are companies like Mice on Ice that provide frozen rodents to owners and pet stores around the world. It makes me smile to know that I was the pioneer in using dead animals, and not torturing live ones. I still have customers who want to feed their monster lizards and snakes live prey, but I strongly discourage it.

I do suppose there will be those who object to feeding snakes live or dead animals because the rodent suffers at some point. That's simply not true. Rodents raised as snake food are treated— and killed—much more humanely than the cows, sheep, pigs, chickens, and turkeys we eat. The mice and rats are raised in cages, fed well; and when it's time to kill them, those cages are wheeled into a room where the oxygen is removed. The rodents faint and die much like someone would from carbon monoxide poisoning.

I also try to impress upon prospective snake and lizard owners that there is an even more dramatic aspect to owning a big reptile. Apart from the fact that a really big one might try to kill you, there is the mess factor. Big snakes don't go to the bathroom for weeks and weeks at a time. Then, usually after the snake sheds its skin, everything they have eaten over the previous weeks just comes tumbling out. What you have is a giant pile of poop that rivals the output of a horse. If they poop inside their cage, they manage to get it all over themselves, and snakes don't have a self-cleaning capacity. It's up to the owner. The smell is almost impossible to describe, but just imagine everything the snake has eaten—undigested rodent hair and other sundry animal parts—all piled up in the middle of the snake's cage.

To this day, I recommend that anyone determined to have a snake consider a nice little ball python, rat snake, corn snake, or king snake. If you want to go bigger, the only two I will recommend are boa constrictors and carpet pythons. Here in New York all large constricting snakes are illegal, because when they become too large for the owner to handle, they end up being dropped off at a pet store like mine or dumped into the wilds somewhere. The Florida Everglades are an excellent example of big snakes gone bad, not only posing a threat to humans when loosed, but threatening an already compromised ecosystem.

Perhaps the bigger question here is why humans are so fascinated by reptiles. Do snakes have the genuine capacity for a relationship with humans? For many, it's the exotic factor or the danger factor or some macho fulfillment. For people like me, it's the fascination with an animal that has no eyelids, no ears, no arms, no legs and only one lung, and that comes in so many variations.

I ask myself why some snakes are venomous and others aren't. For example, if the normal diet for a venomous snake like the rattlesnake and the mamba is a mouse, why does the snake need venom? From an evolutionary viewpoint, I suppose that the snakes with the most potent venom could kill rodents the fastest, which means they got to eat faster and better. So maybe it's a matter of survival and prevailing over other reptiles.

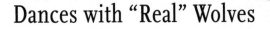

CHAPTER 21

Dances with "Real" Wolves

Survival is something that wolves know well. Wolves have always fascinated me and I wanted to learn about them up close and personal. Every time I looked at a dog, I was intrigued by how that particular breed had evolved from some ancient wolf. How did we go from lupus to Lhasa apso? What could I learn from living around modern-day wolves?

At that time, I was appearing on television on a regular basis, educating the public about the world of animals. Because of that, the government was able to give me a permit to keep wolves for educational purposes. My permit required that I create a suitable enclosure for the wolves that would keep the public safe from my animals. I complied with every requirement, and then I was ready to get my first wolf.

There were at the time breeders who were allowed to breed and sell wolves for both movie work and educational purposes. I bought a female puppy and brought her home. I named her Twinkums. My dog Barney was actually the one who raised her. She believed she was the alpha wolf, but Barney had other ideas. Growling, snarling, grabbing, and biting, Barney exercised total domination over her until she finally had to submit. That was a good thing, because the full-grown wolf is twice as big as a dog like Barney. If he didn't exercise complete domination, he could have been injured or killed when the wolf was full grown. Eventually, I got a second wolf that I named Frosty, and Barney repeated the same training with him. All Barney had to do was give them that "look," and they'd roll over on their backs and submit to him.

Feeding the wolves taught me the first interesting contrast between wolf and dog. Wolves are obligate carnivores; they need to eat meat, and only meat. If you feed dog food to a wolf, it will become violently ill. That means man somehow modified the original wolf's digestive system so that it could eat other food. If we go back to ancient tribes who kept wolves as pets, the only wolves that survived were those who could tolerate eating hooves and bones when there wasn't enough meat. The surviving wolves produced litters that were eventually able to thrive even without meat in their diet.

What's also interesting is the difference between wolf and dog teeth.

A dog's mouth is a constant source of problems. Their teeth are always developing tartar, rotting, and falling out. The wolf's teeth are amazing. They're like little pieces of ivory beautifully spaced out and strong. A dog's teeth are all crowded, and very often weak. With either of my wolves, I could hook my finger under one of their canine teeth and lift him or her off the ground. The wolf would just hang there by its tooth. That's how well embedded those teeth are in the wolf's mouth.

Training wolves is also another fascinating aspect of their behavior. With a dog, it's either domination or behavior modification through a reward system. Mostly, we train dogs through some degree of domination with a sprinkle of positive reinforcement.

While I did have to dominate my wolves, I could accomplish that by merely turning them over on their backs every now and then. The occasional reminder sufficed. Quite unlike a dog, though, the wolf could not be trained—positive reinforcement or otherwise—to do something it didn't want to do. Going for walks is a good example.

Even though I had a government permit for my wolves, I didn't want to take Barney and a couple of my other dogs, along with the wolves, for a walk during the day—just in case I might upset a neighbor. The wolves had no objection to the leash, but walking at night posed other problems. In particular, if Twinkums saw something she didn't like, she would freeze. She wouldn't go forward and she wouldn't go backward. The only way I could get her home was to pick her up and carry her. So there I was, with at least one dog on a leash and a wolf in my arms.

Wolves also learn very differently than dogs do. Dogs need to be shown something and trained through repetition. Wolves learn from observation. They really are much smarter than dogs.

Take the water faucet. On the side of my house is a spigot with a bucket underneath it. I'd fill the bucket on a regular basis, and the dogs and wolves drank from the bucket. Occasionally, the dogs might lick the spigot or the inside of the bucket if it needed refilling. If the bucket was empty, they'd simply walk away thirsty. The wolves on the other hand would go to the spigot and try to turn it on. Twinkums actually learned how to do that. This of course made the dogs very happy. The problem was that she didn't know how to turn it off—or she didn't want to, which didn't make me happy at all. From her perspective, fresh water was always flowing. So I had to install a key on the spigot so she couldn't turn it on at will.

She could also open doors. Sure, Lassie could open doors by turning the doorknob, but it was her trainer, Rudd Weatherwax, who taught her how to do that. My wolves learned to do that by watching me. When my dogs wanted to go outside, they would scratch at the door until I opened it. If I didn't open it, they'd give up and go lie down somewhere else. If Twinkums wanted to go outside, she would turn the knob and open the door. Again, the dogs benefited from her powers of observation.

One of my longtime mentors and good friends was Roger Caras, who studied wolves in great detail. I did several television shows with him, and I took my wolves with me. Roger was amazed at how well trained they were. Truthfully, I was the one who was well trained—by them. I never forced them to do anything they didn't want to do. If they didn't want to do something, or didn't think it was amusing, they just wouldn't respond. The fact that I didn't force them to do anything they didn't like transformed them into much more agreeable animals.

I remember watching the movie *Dances with Wolves* and observing the "well-trained wolf" named Two-Socks. In fact, Two-Socks was a wolf-dog hybrid that favored the wolf side in its appearance. Rarely do you see a full-blooded wolf in a performing mode. Most of the performing "wolves" are wolf-husky hybrids.

Perhaps my biggest surprise living around real wolves was discovering how shy they were. If a stranger came into my house, the wolves would hide—not out of fear, but out of shyness. My dogs, on the other hand, would somehow determine whether or not the stranger was friendly, and then respond either with wagging tails or menacing growls. The dog, most likely because of thousands of years of domestication, can feel obligated to protect the house.

The wolf feels no such obligation. As long as there is no threat from someone, they slink away.

Another interesting difference between wolves and dogs is that wolves see every other animal as prey. Over the years, dogs have learned to socialize with horses, cows, sheep, chickens, geese, ducks, turkeys, rabbits, cats, and a host of other animals. For a wolf, all of those animals are potential prey. One of the strangest interactions I ever saw between my wolves and another animal involved a bobcat I had named Coco. At the same time I studied wolves, I was also studying wild cats, and I had a few of them. The wild cats were allowed in the house, where the wolves were only allowed to come into the den from their outside enclosure. The "wolf den" was reasonably chew-proof. The walls were made out of brick and the furniture was sturdy. Of course, I didn't have a child at the time, so I didn't have to worry about any of those issues. I can't imagine how early man kept wolves around their small children. A few hits to the head of a pet wolf hungrily eyeing a child must have been an important step in domestication.

So, there I'd be, sitting on the couch, and Coco would crouch down in the opening between the den and the kitchen. Twinkums would come in, see the bobcat, and put her face just inches away from the cat's face. Both would stare at each other without moving, each wanting to kill the other, but they didn't. It seemed that they recognized each other as equals, and it was simply a matter of "facing off." In all the ten years that I had the wolves, no battles ever occurred.

The only "battle" involved Twinkums and me. One day, I reached down to pet her, and suddenly she lifted her head up—hard. The top of her head hit my jaw, smashing my teeth together. I still have a chip in one of my teeth from that playful encounter. Twinkie, as I often called her, loved to play; I just had to be careful. Her favorite thing was fireflies. I'd watch her outside at night, jumping high into the air trying to catch the insects. Wolves also like water, and Twinkie was no exception. I even built a big concrete pond for her and Frosty; and they would play in that pond for hours at a time. I would never have believed that if I hadn't lived with them.

I was also surprised to learn that wolves only breed once a year, both males and females, and only during springtime. In the dog world, there are only three breeds that come into season once a year: the basenji, the New Guinea singing dog, and the dingo. Those three breeds must be closer to their wild wolf origins.

At this point I should mention that I did at one time adopt what was called a wolf-dog hybrid that had been confiscated by the local authorities. I was curious to see how it would behave with both full-blooded wolves and dogs. In fact, this animal is not a hybrid at all. A hybrid is a cross between two different species. Wolves and dogs are the same species. People who cross wolves and dogs think they're going to get a dog that looks like a wolf. Instead, they get an animal with the worst characteristics of each breed. What's created isn't a hybrid; it's an abomination.

If a wolf-dog sees a stranger, instead of hiding like a true wolf, it becomes protective and starts to act aggressive. Given that the wolf is twice the size of most dogs with jaws and teeth to match, there is now real danger for both the owner and the stranger. Once I realized how dangerous my wolf-dog was, I had him euthanized. He represented a violation of twenty thousand years of selective breeding to produce dogs that lived amicably with humans. .

Most of what I know about wolves is from firsthand experience, augmented by the vast knowledge of people like Roger Caras.
What most impressed me during those ten years "dancing with
wolves" was how intelligent they are. While there are no cognitive
studies detailing their level of intelligence, as there are for dolphins,
chimps, parrots, and other animals, I would have to say that wolves
are certainly among the top three or four.

CHAPTER 22

What Has Spots Like a Leopard but Isn't a Leopard?

Where crossing wolves and dogs may produce a hybrid with the worst characteristics of the species, breeding domestic cats with Asian leopard cats (*Felis bengalis*) produces a beautiful and docile pet called the Bengal cat. As many people know, the common domestic cat evolved from the North African wild cat. The first generation of hybrids produced from the Asian leopard cat combined characteristics of both African and Asian species. What the first generation of Asian/domestic kittens didn't have was any of the domesticated cat's temperament; what they did have was the DNA for the spotted coat of the wild animal. In successive generations, fertile hybrids were bred back to the domesticated cat, thus producing kittens that were three parts domesticated cat and one part wild animal. Additional crossbreeding ultimately changed that ratio to one part wild and seven parts domesticated. Once the breeder goes back four or five generations, the animal is deemed domesticated.

My personal experience with Bengal cats stemmed from my fascination with Asian leopard cats that were bottle raised from infancy in private collections. Given that leopard spots were the sought-after characteristic, those of us attempting to breed for that trait—along with breeding out any wild behavior—chose Abyssinian cats because of their solid colors—ruddy, red, blue, and cream—against which the spots would stand out more dramatically. It took several generations of breeding before the spots "migrated" from the belly to the top of the cat. The result today is a Bengal cat with exotic coloring and a sweet disposition. Even though they are fully domesticated, Bengal cats cannot be exported to other countries without a CITES permit because Asian leopard cats are an endangered species, along with margays and ocelots; and the authorities are afraid that wild spotted cats will be traded internationally as Bengal cats.

Another hybrid cat that is currently being bred is the Savannah cat, which is a cross between a domesticated cat and a serval. The serval looks like a small cheetah, weighs about forty pounds, and isn't especially fierce. In the wild, they mostly hunt small birds and rodents, so they're not as aggressive as the lynx or bobcat. At present, Savannah cats are almost totally domesticated, and the breeders are working to fine-tune both the spotting and the personality. Those breeders might do well to consider the words of Roger Caras in his book *A Perfect Harmony: The Intertwining Lives of Animals and Humans Throughout History*:

> *Because it is a recent domestication, we may not yet have a real handle on the cat's genetic potential. Except for the occasional obese specimen or freak, all domestic cats weigh in at about the same, give or take two or three pounds. . . . Horses run from very small ponies to massive draft animals of almost a ton in weight. If that kind of variation is ever achieved in the domestic cat, we*

will have to do some careful reevaluation of its roles in our lives. A feral tabby cat the size of a large leopard or jaguar . . . would have lost most of its fear, and fear of man is the only thing that enables man and large predators to co-exist. . . . It may be a consideration for the future.

Considering that Savannah cats arrived on the scene shortly after 1996, after Roger's book was written and he had died, it's interesting to speculate what he would have said about their evolution. The domestic cat weighs around ten pounds, Bengals around fifteen, while the Savannah comes from crossbreeding with a thirty- to forty-pound serval. Larger, more powerful hybrids might pose a genuine threat to humans, beauty and spots aside.

A good example of "wild gone bad" can be seen with keeping lynxes as pets. Averaging forty pounds, servals and caracal lynxes are legal to keep in many parts of the United States. These are not cats that one can keep loose in the house. These are also cats that, if bottle raised, will love their owner beyond all measure of loyalty, including protecting their owner from anyone else who comes in contact. Having company over may be problematic, or worse. The lynx, serval, or bobcat, all of which I have owned and raised, will hiss and snarl at the "intruder." There is also a real and constant danger of outright attack upon the unsuspecting mailman or plumber. Furthermore, there is no recognized rabies vaccine for these wild cats. Vacations are a thing of the past because no one will "cat-sit" for you. Your exotic, wild cat will permanently live in the land of "no," as you watch your house become compromised or destroyed. The cat will see your house as its habitat, and you will see your life forever changed.

One of my dearest friends, John, an art dealer and keeper of exotic animals, did have a caracal lynx that he treasured and pampered. While she was still young, he allowed her to live in the house with both him and his wife. I was able to meet the cat when he called to ask me a favor.

"Marc, do you think you could make a trip over here and trim my lynx's nails?"

I knew there were no local veterinarians willing to perform such a task. At first I hesitated. "I guess I could. All right, I'll do it for you."

I knew that my friend would pay me very well for my time. That wasn't the issue. How was I going to accomplish this? I got an idea.

"Here's what you need to do. Put a leash on the lynx and lock it in the bathroom. I'll figure it out from there."

With that, I headed for his house and arrived to find myself greeted by a forty-pound hissing, snarling wild animal. This might be harder than I had thought it would be.

"What shall we do? What shall we do?"

My friend sounded desperate, but I was hatching another idea.

"Okay, your wife can handle the cat pretty well. Have your wife put the leash on the cat, and we'll all make the animal run into the bathroom. We'll close the door, and then I'll go inside. I'll slide the leash under the door, and you can pull it tight so that the cat is held against the door until I get inside. Once in there, I can sit on top of the cat and trim the nails."

Into the bathroom I went, undaunted by all the hissing and snarling. I inched closer and closer until I was able to scratch its head. Rather quickly, the cat began to purr and relax. I thought to myself, "Well, this seems a little too easy," and with that I picked up one of its paws. I gently squeezed out the claws and begin to trim the nails, just as I would with a house cat. Outside the door, I could hear my friend's worried voice.

"Marc, is everything all right?"

While John would in the future become a close friend, he was at that time someone I knew only professionally and I wanted to impress him.

"Yes, John, I'm fine. I've got everything under control."

I was thinking to myself that this was far too easy. How was I going to charge him for such a simple task? Another idea.

"John, here's what we'll do. I'm going to slide the leash back under the door, and I want you to pull as hard as you can."

As I took the leash off the cat, I could easily imagine John getting ready for the tug of his life. I slid the leash under the door and grabbed hold of my end with both hands, bracing my feet wide apart on the floor.

I heard him bang up against the door.

"Quick, John. Pull!"

I could hear him grunting and pulling, while I was pulling with all of my might on the other side of the door. If a lynx could laugh, I'm sure this one would have.

Finally deciding that I had earned my fee and his respect, I pulled back the leash and put it back on the cat. Then I messed up my hair, pulled my shirt out of my pants, and opened the door.

Staggering out, I proudly announced, "It's all right. I got the nails cut."

"Oh, thank God! Are you okay?"

He was sweating like a river, and I felt a little bad about my ruse.

"Please, please. What do I owe you?"

"Don't worry, John. No charge; it's on the house."

A couple of months later, after we had gotten to know each other much better, I told him the truth and he laughed. The lynx eventually moved to his private zoo in Africa, where she lived a semiwild life in a spacious enclosure that he built for her. Every night she would run into the bush, and she would return the next morning. For several years during those outings, she mated with truly wild caracal lynxes and bore many offspring. Ultimately, a leopard killed her while she was out of her safe enclosure.

She lived a wild life. She died a wild death.

CHAPTER 23

Domestic Partners

Living wild is where every captive animal began, whether wild-caught or domestically raised. My friend's wild lynx would never have become domesticated, regardless of the training or attention he bestowed upon her. No amount of "love" would have transformed her from a wild animal into an animal whose memory of being wild had been erased. The case of Siegfried and Roy and the attack of the white tiger is an excellent example of this. That tiger was raised in captivity, trained, and kept resident around both men. The tiger was affectionate and responsive. To many who have watched footage of Siegfried and Roy at home with their big cats, that is exactly what many people believed to be true: they were watching big "cats." Nothing could be further from the truth.

It's not surprising that people who watch performing animals, and also those who observe firsthand those animals who live with humans as pets, would believe that these animals have become domesticated. Chimpanzees, so often seen on television and in movies, are an important case in point.

What happened in 2008 in Connecticut to the woman who treated her chimpanzee like a human partner is an important case. She raised that chimp from birth, bonded with it, and the chimp seemed to behave like a polite little human—until some unknown trigger caused it to go off on the woman's friend and nearly kill her. Sure, a lot of people are saying it must have been the combination of Xanax and wine, or it was the friend's new hairstyle, but that's ridiculous. A wild animal doesn't need an excuse to act wild. That's why people who choose to have a wild animal, whether or not it's been raised in captivity from birth, need to create a habitat for that animal that is separate from the human's habitat. Then, the human can go visit the animal in its home. The boundaries are clear for both, and neither one will be compromised. I would never sleep with a chimpanzee or other wild animal. I'd be terrified of having a bad dream, disturbing the sleeping animal, and waking up with missing body parts. I'm all about sharing knowledge, useful knowledge. Maybe someone reading this will now think twice before trying to live with a so-called "domestic" animal that is really wild.

"Christian the Lion" is a more positive example of someone living successfully with a wild animal—up to a point. Back in the 1960s, when virtually any animal could be bought and sold, an advertisement in the Harrods catalog caught the attention of John Rendall and Anthony "Ace" Bourke. Beguiled by a cute little lion cub, they promptly bought him and christened him, ironically, Christian. Unlike the lions and the Christians, this namesake was pampered and raised to become almost like a very big cat. At a certain point, the owners realized their pet had become too large and "wild" to manage, and they released him in Africa to live out his life as a truly wild animal. It was never made clear if Christian learned how to hunt like a truly wild lion, or if the owners arranged for him to be fed "just in case." Certainly, he continued to live happily ever after; and of course, YouTube has memorialized forever that tearful reunion of man and beast.

The cats we consider domesticated are in fact the only animals that can move between both worlds. A pet cat can disappear into the forest and live there for the rest of its life—or it can return home, your home or someone else's, and resume its pet status.

In sharp contrast to cats and lions, wild-caught parrots and those born in captivity are genetically the same birds. The bred parrot's behavior and habits are still those of the wild bird, as anyone who lives with parrots will attest. The only difference between the bird in the wild and the bird in your living room is that the bird in your hand has no fear of humans. If you are in the jungles of Central America and surprise a macaw, it will promptly fly off. If you confront the macaw in your living room, he may very well rush at your feet, wings spread and beak ready to strike.

A domesticated animal is one whose genes are controlled by man. A parrot, like the macaw, is genetically the same bird that is flying around in the wilds of South America. It acts the same and looks the same, and its behavior and habits remain those of the wild bird. The big difference is that if you turn that bird loose in an unfamiliar place, it may not have the necessary tools to survive. However, if you take a macaw egg from a captive pair and put it in a wild macaw's nest, it will absolutely be able to survive when raised by the foster parents.

In contrast, a dog is a domesticated wolf. If your dog escapes and becomes lost, unless he can find food from humans, he may very well starve. He might join up with other dogs and become part of a pack, and the pack might even kill and eat the occasional other animal in order to survive. They haven't reverted to being wild; they're simply renegades. They cannot reverse their domestication and become truly wild animals. They need some kind of human intervention to survive, even if it's only a garbage dump to pick through.

Other birds that we keep as pets are also fascinating examples of domestication over thousands of years. The original wild canary was about four inches long and brown in color. Then one yellow bird born in captivity was a spontaneous mutation, and humans started breeding yellows to yellows, presumably because the yellows were considered prettier. Then a white bird was born, and we started breeding whites to whites and whites to yellows. We ultimately created a rainbow effect for canaries. It's not just about color. Years and years of confinement also brought about a certain kind of contentment for canaries, which can also be said of finches and parakeets. While some people would say that no bird should be caged, these small birds are truly content in their cages—as long as they're well fed and their cages are kept clean. How do we know this? They sing. Canaries sing because they're happy; and only the males sing. They sing to attract a mate; and if the bird thinks its cage is an ideal nest, he will sing to attract a female.

Our domestication of pigeons is similar to that of canaries. Apparently, the original "owners" didn't like the rather dull appearance of their first pigeons, so they began crossbreeding color anomalies until a new "rainbow" of colors was produced. Pigeons today have remarkable colorations and are widely collected for those variations.

Then of course we have our popular dogs. Why do some dogs have floppy ears and others have pointed ears that stand up? All the breed differences we see today originated with ancient tribes that bred their wolves for certain characteristics. We're still experimenting today, producing new breeds all the time.

Sometimes people stop experimenting with different breed characteristics. This is especially true of macaws. For a while, breeders were crossing blue and golds with scarlet macaws and producing catalinas or green wings. What they discovered was something I always thought to be true. The two original color combinations are the most beautiful. The others look a little bit like bad tie-dye.

Now the ferret, which, contrary to popular belief, is not a big rodent, is the domesticated version of the Eurasian polecat; but it neither looks like nor behaves like its wild relatives.

Cows are a domesticated version of the auroch. The pig is a domesticated version of the wild boar. The hamster we keep as a pet is not at all like its wild cousin in Syria, whence all hamsters originate. Even guinea pigs in America bear almost no resemblance to their relatives in South America. The same is true of the domestic rabbit, which is nothing like the European wild rabbit.

Humans selectively bred all of these farm and pet animals until no wildness was left. Someone's cute little hamster would last about two minutes in the wild. Other animals, such as pigs, goats, and even horses, are more like cats. They can go back and forth between wild and domesticated living. So in fact we have three groups of pet animals: truly domesticated animals, wild animals that have been bred in captivity, and wild-caught animals that are kept in captivity. Only the first group is genuinely safe to live with.

What it all comes down to is control versus domestication. Look at wild elephants. In Asia, specially trained elephant handlers called mahouts will go out into the wilds and catch an elephant. He'll bring it back to the village and chain it up, and a mahout will teach it to do all kinds of tasks. The mahout will live with that elephant for the rest of its life, and the elephant will obey him. He's controlling a wild animal. The owner of a herding sheepdog will get a puppy, train it to herd sheep, and stay with that dog for the rest of its life. He has trained a dog that was already domesticated. If the mahout is careless with his elephant's chains, the elephant will lumber back into the jungle and resume its wild life. If the sheepherder loses his dog, the dog is at the mercy of the elements.

The elephant in the room is an apt reminder of what domesticated really means.

CHAPTER 24

Smiley, the One-Toothed Monkey

Monkeys are never domesticated. Despite the people who think they're cute, monkeys really don't make good pets unless you create a special habitat for them. Then you can visit them in their home whenever you want to, and your house won't be destroyed. When you try to bring a monkey into your house, it doesn't work because monkeys—like parrots—don't understand restrictions on their basic movements. People who get a monkey when it's a baby think that it will grow up to be just like a little person, but it won't. It will always be half monkey and half human, which is even worse than pure monkey.

The reason I know so much about monkeys is that I followed the example of Gerald Durrell, who learned about animals by observing them firsthand. It has never been about selling monkeys, or any other kind of animal; it has always been about pursuing a dream. Someday I wanted to be able to share all of my knowledge with others, to help humans become better humans by understanding what we share in common with animals—and what we don't. For example, in the animal world random events are the norm. Animals accept that randomness; and as Walt Whitman once wrote, "they do not whine or complain." Human beings are obsessed with finding answers to everything. "Why do bad things happen to good people?" "Why do good things happen to bad people?" We are obsessed with finding those answers, and all too often we make our lives miserable searching for the impossible.

This is why I love to reach out to people through radio, television, personal appearances, and now books. I have something to share, and I am driven to share that knowledge.

Keeping monkeys and buying monkeys and selling monkeys was my way of learning about them. I couldn't learn that from a book. I had to be bitten and scratched and peed on to gain that knowledge. I have scars all over my body to prove it. Most people don't realize how serious a monkey bite can be. Anyone who thinks monkeys are cute and cuddly has never been around one. And if one of them decides it wants to kill you, it wants to kill you. That sad example in Connecticut is a good example of a "tame, gentle" monkey reverting to its wild nature. Chimpanzees in particular may have sweetly human faces, but they are most certainly not human.

Back in the 1970s and '80s, monkeys were commonly kept in people's homes, and the monkey business was huge. One particular monkey breeder came to me and wanted to have me sell five capuchin monkeys for him. I happened to have someone looking for capuchins, so I agreed to handle the deal. I was still learning a lot about monkeys. In those days, there wasn't much information about monkey behavior in captivity or as pets, so everyone was still on a long learning curve. Today, given the knowledge I have acquired about monkeys, I would only sell one to someone who understands that a monkey cannot live in a human habitat. Tree branches and fine furniture are all the same to a monkey, and there isn't enough air freshener in the world to eliminate the odor of a simian. The only way to "own" a monkey is to create a habitat just for him, and then visit him in his world.

But in that moment, I found myself with four female capuchins and one male named Smiley. All too soon I would find out the deep irony of his name.

I arranged to have all five monkeys shipped to my store on Long Island, and I set aside a large cage, ten feet high by eight feet wide, to be their home for a week or so before I shipped them to the buyer in another state. The females were named Mongo, Samantha, Peanuts, and Sammy. Smiley was a big, tough guy with a very strange history. He had been named Smiley because whoever owned him before the breeder had tried to keep him from biting by extracting his canine teeth. The veterinarian had only been able to extract three of those, leaving behind the fourth, the roots of which were so deep that it couldn't be extracted. Now Smiley had a perpetual snarl with this one tooth sticking out, and in the first moments I observed him it was clear that his goal in life was to kill somebody. I had already been warned that more than once he had tried to act on this goal; he was one of the few monkeys with hopes and aspirations. As a rule, animals don't have hopes and aspirations, but Smiley did: to kill a human being.

Despite his three missing teeth, he still had plenty of others, along with a lot of power and muscle, even though he weighed only fifteen pounds. That may not sound like much, but when a monkey is enraged, every one of those pounds becomes super-energized, plus a monkey can use his feet like hands. So you have powerful jaws and four strong arms coming at you from all angles. I had always respected monkeys, but my limited knowledge had not prepared me for Smiley.

The day came for me to take the monkeys to the airport, and I had the travel carriers all set. I had also created a trapdoor in the big cage so that each monkey came out one at a time, and then I could grab it and put it into the individual travel cage. Monkeys always look for ways to escape from their cages, so as long as the monkey didn't see me opening the trapdoor, I was able to capture each one as it bolted for freedom.

Everything was set; I got the carriers ready and then went to the big cage and unlocked, but didn't open, the door. Just as I did so, the phone rang and I turned around to answer it. It was six-thirty in the morning, which meant it was either one of my employees or my wife. It was an employee saying he would be late, and so I was off the phone in no more than a couple of minutes. I turned around and saw to my horror that the little door was no longer just unlocked; it was wide open.

There was Smiley sitting on the floor looking straight at me, with the four girls behind him. All five had murder in their eyes.

"Hello, guys," I said cautiously. "Who wants a banana?"

The banana ploy wasn't working, and then suddenly all five of them zoomed at me, covering my body in mad monkeys. I felt a little like Godzilla in one of those Japanese movies where he's being attacked by several smaller monsters.

Oh, my god, I thought. I could die.

My only hope, and indeed my ultimate salvation, was that I was dressed in a ski jacket that covered my wrists and neck. At least the monkeys wouldn't be able to open up any arteries.

I dropped to the ground and began to crawl toward the big cage, my back covered in screaming, biting monkeys. My plan was to grab each one and stuff it back through the little door and into the cage. Bleeding and in pain, I managed to get the four females back inside the enclosure, but there was still Smiley.

I grabbed for him but he jumped away, landing about six feet from me. He looked at me with that awful grimace that only a capuchin can produce, and it was clear that he and I were about to do battle. King Kong versus Godzilla.

Just like in the movies, we rushed at each other and I found myself fighting for my life against a fifteen-pound monkey. Finally, I managed to get him around the throat and began to choke him— to death, if necessary. Anyone who might judge me for that has never encountered a bloodthirsty monkey.

I was gaining power over him, and the adrenaline in my veins was so strong that I might indeed have choked him to death. Then I remembered myself, and somehow I managed to put him into his travel carrier and lock him securely inside.

Now I had a new problem. I couldn't go to the airport looking torn up and bloody, and if I went to the hospital, I'd be in all the major newspapers. My doctor friend wasn't at all surprised to get my call; he'd been tending my wounds for years. He came right over and stitched me up in the store. Half an hour later I was on my way to the airport, both hands in huge bandages.

All ended well for the monkeys, who finally ended up in Texas with a respected breeder who was pleased with all of the offspring they produced. The monkeys were no worse for the battle and were happy to live an uncaged life.

That was my big lesson about monkeys beyond just respecting their wildness. Given the opportunity, even the most docile monkey will revert to some primitive instinct, and we as humans cannot possibly know when that might happen. Certainly, those who study and work with monkeys may be more tuned in to those "wild" signals, but the average pet owner has no instinct for when such an event could occur.

Smiley wasn't a bad monkey; he was just a monkey with an unfortunate history, and, cage aside, he was still a wild animal behaving out of instinct.

CHAPTER 25

Into My Arms, into My Heart:
Georgette the Baboon

"Listen, I'm really sorry that I can't pay you what I owe you. Would you be willing to accept a baboon instead? She's probably worth about a thousand dollars, and I'll even pay to ship her to you."

Dave was a good guy, and I'd done considerable business with him over the years. Still, I really didn't want a baboon, and I didn't know if I'd be able to sell it in order to recoup the money I was owed. But I definitely had a soft spot for monkeys.

"Okay, Dave, go ahead and send her. I'll figure something out."

Several days later, I went to the airport to pick her up. I had already found a breeder in Texas who sold baboons to zoos, and he was fairly sure he would be able to find her a permanent home.

There she was, in a huge wooden box big enough for a gorilla. Memories of Smiley made me wonder how I was going to deal with this. I decided it was best to be prepared for whatever might happen, so I came back with a baseball bat, a crowbar, and a hammer. And a sturdy cage. All I could hear inside the box was a low grunt, grunt, grunt.

"So, you're going to put her in there?" The attendant looked a little nervous himself.

"Sure," I answered back, but I wasn't sure at all. "Let me see what I'm up against."

With that, I pried open the box with the crowbar, and out zoomed an olive-colored flash of fur that quickly disappeared into the back room, where she hid underneath a table. I rushed after her, not knowing what to expect next. Weighing between fifteen and twenty pounds, she was certainly as strong as or stronger than Smiley had been. Then came the surprise.

She looked at me and I looked at her, neither one of us moving. Suddenly she spread out her arms toward me and jumped into my arms, wrapping herself around my neck while she kissed me and began to cry. What I "heard" was her entire life saga about being captured in Africa and being brought here. My heart melted, and I could no longer think about selling her. She had touched a chord in my heart. I lived a solitary life except for my animals; no wife or children at that point in my life, and this animal had offered me—by any definition, one of her "captors"—complete adulation. I named her Georgette and took her back to my store.

Her new home was a very large cage in the middle of my store, where she could be around the other animals but, most important, be around me. That soon became the problem. She adored me and I believed she would have died for me. Over the years she gradually perceived everyone else as a potential threat to my safety. Her mood changed and she lived in a state of perpetual agitation because she was always worried that something was going to happen to me. I adored her because of that devotion, and I was heartsick over having to think about finding her a new home.

Fortunately for both of us, one of my friends, who lived only five minutes away and who was and still is a true monkey nut with three baboons of his own, agreed to let her live with him. Still, it took me two years to give her up. When I finally did, she accepted her new home and the other monkeys as if she had always belonged there. To this day, she still lives five minutes away, and I go to visit her often. We hug and kiss, and I don't think about the fact that she weighs sixty pounds and has the strength of four Smileys. She lives in a monkey habitat, and I'm her human soul mate.

Forever.

CHAPTER 26

Baby on Board: Sweet Jessie

Not all soul mates are pleasant to be around. Monkeys smell. Not just a mildly unpleasant musty smell but enough to make you pass out. I knew that, but it was my experience with tamarins, a species related to marmosets, that revealed just how nasty monkey odor can be.

Someone came into my store about "two" tamarins, a male and a female, that he wanted me to sell for him. I knew a breeder in Florida so I agreed to keep them in my store until I could arrange for their transport.

When he brought them in, there were actually five tamarins, not two, huddled inside their sleeping box with the entrance covered so as not to spook them. Tamarins are very small, only about the size of your hand, and I wasn't afraid to open the box and take them out in order to move them to a bigger cage.

The smell of them stopped my breath, and I had to remind myself that in a bigger space, the stench could be reduced to merely odor. I decided not to put them near my newest monkey, a lovely, young Patas female whom I had named Jessie when I had acquired her three years earlier. Unlike the majority of monkeys, Patas monkeys do not smell and are one of the most beautiful monkeys in the world. Considered an "old world" monkey, they come from Africa, as do macaques, guenons, and baboons. "New world" monkeys come from Central and South America, breeds such as tamarins, marmosets, squirrel monkeys, capuchins, spider monkeys, and howlers.

I had gotten Jessie as a tiny baby and bottle-raised her, after going through a succession of guenons and macaques; but it was the Patas that I had aspired to. Gerald Durrell had collected them as well, and praised both their beauty and intelligence. Because I had become Jessie's surrogate mother, I took her everywhere I went, including my new cable television show on Long Island. She literally grew up on a television set, and she would play with all the other animals I was featuring. I always knew that she couldn't stay with me forever. Eventually, she would have become psychologically warped by not being able to "protect" me from everyone who came into the store, and she would not be able to integrate with the rest of the monkeys. Now, she had five new tamarins to visit with until it was time to ship them to their new home.

The day finally came for Jessie to move on, and it was with my good breeder friend in Florida that she found her new home, and she has had four babies in the last fifteen years. She still lives there today, happy in her surroundings and captured forever on television. YouTube has extensive footage of her and me performing, and she lives on in my memory.

It needs to be said that not all monkeys are horrible and bad; you just have to treat them like monkeys. Georgette and Jessie were unusual, but I still wouldn't have allowed them to live in my house. If we understand and honor the nature of animals, we will probably understand more about ourselves as humans. Learning to see the world from an animal's point of view can offer insights about the world of humans. Through them, with them, we are embracing both our past and our future.

CHAPTER 27

Pigs in Paradise,
Not in Your Living Room

*B*abe is an illusion. The cute pig everyone fell in love with on the big screen was in fact a series of baby pigs that still looked pink and adorable. Full-grown pigs, including the ever-popular Vietnamese pot-bellied pig, are big and demanding as pets.

It is indeed true that pigs are probably the smartest domesticated animals. Domesticated, not tame, like parrots that some people believe are domesticated. Parrots are not domesticated, at least not yet. Some day, with continued breeding—as was done with wolves—we may end up with domesticated parrots, but we're not there yet. What always impresses me most about pigs is the hypocrisy surrounding them. On the one hand, humans acknowledge that pigs are way up on the intelligence scale; on the other hand, we torture pigs more than any other animal raised for food. The belief that pigs are dirty is a myth. They relieve themselves in one place, and keep themselves very, very clean. The "dirty" myth comes from the fact that pigs don't sweat; so when they're hot, they roll around in the mud or dirt in order to stay cool. If too many pigs are confined in a small area, those poor animals are forced to wallow in their own waste. So we label them "dirty" and allow ourselves to abuse them.

Unlike cattle and even chickens, pigs as a species do not lend themselves to intensive management. They can't be driven like cattle or cooped like chickens, so instead we warehouse them in what amount to jails. In kinder times, a pig farmer would have one boar and three or four sows. This compact pig family would go off into the woods during the day and come back at night to be locked up in the safety of their pens. The pigs would forage in the woods—we can thank them for the luxury of truffles—and round out their diet with whatever the farmer fed them. Every spring, each sow would have maybe ten piglets; the farmer would castrate the males, and when those males were around five months old, the farmer would butcher them as humanely as possible. Then the cycle would start all over again. No one thought of pigs as pets. They were farm animals being raised for meat.

With the advent of media creations like Babe, people became interested in pigs as pets. Who wouldn't want a cute little "Babe" running around their living room? Baby pigs are cute because they have big eyes, a domed forehead, and a little nose. Just like human babies. People are attracted to babies' faces; that attraction is called neoteny. So people in search of a more unusual pet think they're adopting a porcine person. When the piglet grows up, its eyes seem small, its nose becomes a snout, and its face grows very long. In short, it's no longer cute.

Pigs just aren't pretty people. Enter the pot-bellied pig.

In the 1970s, probably as an outgrowth of the Vietnam War, a smaller type of pig was imported into the United States from Canada. Originating in Vietnam, this small pig was not only raised for food, but also was kept as a pet in many households. The first import arrived in Indonesia, then went to Canada, and on into California. I bought some of the first ones in 1978, and I was fascinated. I acquired them not only to sell, but also to keep. As with wolves, I wanted to learn about them firsthand.

My fascination with pigs probably began with a famous animal trainer named Frank Inn, who trained the dog Benji and the pig Arnold, who starred on the television series *Green Acres*. Even as a child, I knew that Arnold was smart, and I wondered what it would be like to have my own little Arnold. Not really little, of course. A full-grown pig weighs between three and four hundred pounds. A full-grown pot-bellied pig still averages eighty to one hundred fifty pounds. Not a tiny porker.

To begin with, the "small, cute" stage doesn't last. When full grown, the pot-bellied pig is the size of a large dog. It's true that one could let the pig live in the house and train it to eliminate outside, but that doesn't change the reality of a pig in the house. The pig is not a graceful animal; and if it rolls around in the dirt outside, that dirt will come back into the house. The pig is also a prodigious eater. In nature, the pig never knows where its next meal will come from, so it eats anything it can find and it doesn't have an "off" button. The pig never thinks it's full. The pig owner compounds the problem by feeding the animal high-calorie food, and soon the pig becomes too heavy. Now the pet owner has a too-big pig who's eating him out of house and home. The pig is also a high-maintenance pet. It's not so difficult to find a pet sitter for a cat or dog, a hamster or a guinea pig, or even a bird in a cage. To the best of my knowledge, there aren't any "pig sitters" listed in the Yellow Pages.

Having a pig as a pet means creating a special habitat for that pig, a habitat that can be easily monitored and managed. The pig owner can visit the pig in its own happy home and also retain the serenity of the human home.

The real challenge of owning a pig as a pet is that they're so smart. With a dog, the trainer can reward the desired behavior with a pleasant word or two. The bird will respond to eye contact as a reward for good behavior. The pig wants to know what's in it for him. What's in it for him is typically food. The well-trained pig becomes the grossly overweight pig.

Another challenge with pigs is their limited mobility. Anatomically, they're just not built for our human environments. They can't negotiate stairs very well; and the big belly hanging over the too-short legs creates movement issues even on flat ground.

In terms of animal husbandry, owning a pig can be most satisfying. The owner lives in his world; the pig lives in his, and the two can visit each other as much as they want. The problem is that most people who buy pigs as pets don't understand that, and so a sad number of baby pigs acquired as pets are abandoned when they become unmanageable adults. That's why I no longer sell or own pot-bellied pigs, or pigs of any kind, for that matter. They're a lot like monkeys, which I don't sell anymore, either. Monkeys—and even uncaged parrots—see your environment as their environment. A monkey tossing a Ming vase just sees a colorful projectile. A parrot chewing your prized Chippendale just sees wood. A pig foraging about in your kitchen just sees food, and he'll open up cabinets to get to it. In your living room, he'll bull-doze your furniture. Unlike a monkey or a parrot, you can't put a pig back in its cage. There is no escape from the pig-at-home.

Realistically, most pig lovers are better off enjoying their pigs on the big screen, or on someone else's farm.

CHAPTER 28

Prairie Dogs and the Epidemic of Fear

A pig in the living room can quickly become the elephant in the room when it comes to health scares for those of us who export animals. The evolution of the prairie dog trade—from despised vermin to prized pets—met one of those scares head-on.

Historically, farmers and ranchers in the West, especially Texas, hated wild prairie dogs, begrudging the small creatures the grass they ate. In particular, the black-tailed prairie dog was Public Enemy Number One. Presumably, the grass they consumed was depriving sheep and cattle of their fair share. There were also the myths about horses and cattle breaking their legs when they stepped into a prairie dog hole. For thousands of years, prairie dogs burrowed under the plains inhabited by bison and antelopes, apparently not endangering those animals with their burrows. Still, given the much bigger food issue, farmers and ranchers in recent history have poisoned, shot, and stomped on prairie dogs and have flooded and bulldozed their villages in an effort to eradicate them. Somewhere, sometime, a few of the orphaned prairie dog babies must have survived, and a kind person took pity on them. Into someone's house they went, and the rescuer came to realize that the little rodents were very social and made very good pets if they were spayed and neutered. Prairie dogs living with a human family interact with that family as if it were their own. In pet-keeping terms, prairie dogs, although they're rodents, behave more like rabbits when kept as a pet. A new pet trade was born.

It wasn't long before some enterprising trapper offered a few prairie dogs to a buyer in Japan. Given the Japanese love for all things rodent, the prairie dog was an instant hit. Prairie dogs, like ferrets, also have an *anime* look. When they stand up on their back legs, their flat little faces look Japanese. Now it wasn't only Americans buying them as pets; the Japanese created an even higher demand for the cute little rodents. By 1995, six thousand prairie dog babies were being exported yearly to Japan alone, and I was a big part of this export expansion. I also kept prairie dogs as pets. Two of my favorites, Bubbles and Squeak, appeared with me on television for many years. They lived to be eight years old, a long life for prairie dogs.

When the farmers and ranchers saw what was happening in the prairie dog pet business, they reevaluated their view of prairie dogs as pests. They began to see them as commodities. At a selling price of fifty to sixty dollars each, the varmints were worth more alive than dead. In response to the high demand, farmers and ranchers began to fence off prairie dog towns so that the sheep and cattle couldn't forage in the money zone. More good news for prairie dog "ranchers" was that there were no legalities or restrictions for catching them. The wild, wild West, indeed.

The boom went bust in 2003 when an animal importer brought into the United States some Gambian pouched rats from West Africa. Unknown to anyone, the rats had a virus called monkey pox. This particular virus, which has nothing at all to do with monkeys, is a zoonotic virus, which means that it can jump from one animal species to humans. It isn't a deadly virus. If a human contracts it, the result is vague, chicken-pox-like symptoms.

Unfortunately, the importer who brought in the rats housed them next to prairie dogs, and the prairie dogs contracted the virus. The prairie dogs didn't suffer and there were no symptoms to indicate that they were even sick. Sadly, the people who bought these infected prairie dogs caught the virus from them, and the witch hunt was on. All sales were immediately stopped, and the export trade disappeared. Ranchers and farmers went back to shooting, drowning, bombing, gassing, and bulldozing the hapless rodents. My previously booming business came to a sudden halt.

In 2009, nearly six years later, the United States government realized that no humans were dying of monkey pox, lifted the embargo, declaring that anyone who wanted to have a prairie dog as a pet could do so, but the damage had already been done. The Japanese, who constituted a majority of the prairie dog business, switched their attention to ferrets. Prairie dogs were no longer regarded as pets. They were back to being vermin.

In my own business, the prairie dog disaster forced me into a cycle of debt. It wasn't the only time that an epidemic was misunderstood, exaggerated, and devastating to my business.

Still reeling from the prairie dog debacle in 2004, I soon found myself facing another epidemic of fear. I was reading the newspaper one morning and saw that a couple of people in Southeast Asia had died of a disease called "bird flu." Within days, all international bird trade was stopped and my business came to a standstill. Again, it took a number of years for the governments around the world to discover that the panic had been unfounded. For me, those years could not be recaptured, and ultimately I was forced into extreme debt. Today, the bird export trade is strong, but there are definitely more hoops to jump through in order to conduct the business.

Thinking back to the early days of my business in the late seventies, *the* big scare was then known as Newcastle disease. Unlike the pandemics after that, Newcastle is a disease that only birds can get; it doesn't jump to humans. Chickens are especially susceptible and often die from it. Because of the huge trade in chickens for the American table, all birds coming into this country are quarantined even today, despite the fact that occurrences of the disease are exceedingly rare. In the 1970s, outbreaks were very common, and the fear for bird importers was well founded.

Back then, the birds were quarantined, and each one was swabbed and a solution was prepared with the sample. That solution was injected into chicken embryos. If the chickens died, it was presumed that the swabbed bird had Newcastle disease. The "infected" bird was then "depopulated," a euphemism for killed. The great fear was that an infected pet bird might somehow infect a chicken and affect one of our important food sources. After thirty days in quarantine, and if no embryo died, the pet bird was banded and released to the importer. During that time, thousands of birds went through government quarantine.

I had just bought twenty yellow-naped Amazons from a quarantine station in California. Some of the birds were for sale in my store, a few had been sold to a wholesaler in Virginia, and I had sold five or six to another wholesaler in New York. A few days after I had sold nearly half the birds, I noticed that one of the baby

Amazons couldn't hold up his head. The bird seemed happy, but he just couldn't keep his head up. I was puzzled, and I wondered what could make that happen. Then, the hair on the back of my neck stood up. I checked in one of my books and discovered that the disease in question caused paralysis of the neck.

Oh, no. One of the birds I had bought from the quarantine station has Newcastle. What to do?

If any birds outside the quarantine station were found infected, the Department of Agriculture would come out and depopulate the entire population of birds, whether in a zoo, a farm, or a store. The government's position was that they could come in, buy the birds, and then kill them. Sadly, there were some unethical people during this time who used this government program to their advantage, "unloading" less valuable birds by indicating they were infected. I looked around at my pet store, and feared the worst.

If the USDA found out about this bird, they were going to come in here and kill every one of my birds, including Harry and Remus. I was caught on the horns of a dilemma. I knew on the one hand that with the exception of the one bird I knew to be sick, the others had not raised any red flags. At the same time, I am someone who tells the truth. What to do?

First, I decided that I had to get the remaining ten Amazons out of my store. I took those birds to a friend's house, and that part of the problem was solved. Next, I had to round up all the other Amazons I had sold. Presuming the rest would be healthy, I planned to tell the Department of Agriculture that I had bought these twenty birds from the California quarantine station, and I had never brought them into my store. I would disclose that one of them was sick, and I understood that the government would have to depopulate all twenty birds. I wasn't going to lie about the sick bird.

My plan hatched, I called the wholesaler in Virginia and told him to send back all the birds. He made a few calls, called me back, and let me know that of the five birds he had bought from me, he had gotten back four. One of the birds he had sold to a woman who responded that her dog had eaten it. Now I had four birds coming back.

The New York wholesaler had all but one of his birds, and now I had eighteen. Time to call the USDA.

Torn between the absolute truth and the potential destruction of my entire bird population and potentially my business, I hesitantly told the official that I had bought twenty birds, and that two of them had died. I described the head symptom and shared my fear that they were infected with Newcastle. I assured him that the birds had been kept at my friend's house and had never come in contact with the birds in my store. Out came the USDA, away went the birds, and I wiped my brow with a sigh of relief.

That wasn't the end of my problems. Subsequently, the government found out that the test they had been using was throwing false negative results, and many birds released from quarantine were in fact infected. Birds with Newcastle disease popped up all over the country, so now veterinarians were on the lookout for birds banded with an "HH," which all the birds from this quarantine station had been banded with. One of those birds was coming home to roost.

A woman in New York who had bought one of my birds through the wholesaler was told by the pet store that sold her the bird that it might be sick. The store suggested she return the bird, but she refused, instead taking it to a veterinarian to determine whether the bird was really sick. The veterinarian of course saw the "HH" and called the USDA. The USDA called the pet store, and their next stop was Parrots of the World. My entire population of birds was threatened after all.

I had been tipped off to expect their visit, and I was preparing my most sincere negotiation. Instead of just buying my birds and killing them, I suggested that we test every bird in the store; if one of them tested positive, I would understand that all the birds had to be killed. They agreed, but now I had to face a thirty-day waiting period before the test results were known. For thirty days I couldn't buy or sell any birds. Every day during that waiting period I would look at Harry and Coral Ann, knowing I was powerless to save them if any of those tests were positive.

It was also a nightmare dealing with prospective buyers. The best I could do was to ask for a deposit and tell them that their birds would be ready in thirty days or whatever the expiration date was for the test results. I lived each day in a panic.

Testing the birds was no less of a drama. I had more than three hundred birds in my store at the time, and each one had to be grabbed, swabbed, and have its identification number marked down. Three weeks into the waiting period, I got a call from the government indicating that the test results had gone bad. We had to test the birds again. We worked through the night to retest all the birds, and of course I had a new complication to deal with. The date I had given buyers with deposits had to be moved forward by thirty more days. I was living a nightmare.

The second thirty days came and went, and good fortune was on my side. My birds were disease-free. I was safe.

The postscript to all of this occurred ten years later. I had decided to buy a horse, so I went down to Virginia to visit a woman who breeds birds for me, and whose husband is a horse trainer.

"Marc, I'm sure you can find a horse among the thoroughbreds off the track. One of my friends can truck it up to Long Island for you."

She and I went down to the racetrack, and I found a horse I liked. We went back to her house, and the conversation turned to bird diseases, I told her my whole sordid Newcastle's story.

"Well, that's a good story. Why don't you look at that cage over there in the corner?"

There in the cage was a beautiful, healthy, ten-year-old yellow-naped Amazon.

"I bought that bird from one of your wholesalers ten years ago, and he told me that I had to give it back because it might be sick. The bird looked healthy to me and I really liked it. I made up the story about my dog eating it. I took off the band and put it in my jewelry box."

She gave me the band and I put it on the gold chain I wear around my neck. It's still there today, right next to my wedding ring. That bird was the only one alive out of that whole group. I like to believe that the good luck bestowed on that bird could be transferred to me. In so many ways, it already has been.

PART IV

ON THE AIR WITH MARTHA STEWART

CHAPTER 29

Discovered!

It was monkey business that got me into show business. Back in the 1980s, animal talent agencies knew I had a baby baboon, and I started to get calls for a cute monkey to appear in some advertisements. Georgette was becoming somewhat famous, and the next thing I knew I got a call from an agent who wanted me to take her onto *Live with Regis and Kathie Lee*. That was twenty years ago. The appearance went fine, and I really connected with the show's producer, Barbara Fight. After a while, the show stopped doing animal segments, and so Barbara and I went our separate ways. Those first segments were almost terrifying, but I decided that television could be an interesting part of my world.

In 1989, after I was finished with that show, I got a call from a man named Arthur Freud, who owned *American Caged-Bird Magazine,* which has since gone out of business. He asked if I could take a few parrots with me to a local Cablevision studio here on Long Island. At that time, it was probably the largest cable hookup in the tristate area, reaching millions of homes. One of those cable shows was called *The Family Pet,* and the host was a very pleasant veterinarian named Dr. Jonathan Greenfield. When Dr. Greenfield invited Arthur to appear on his show with some of Arthur's parrots, that was a problem for Arthur because his parrots were too shy. He and I had been friends for a long time, and so he asked me if I would take some of my birds. I agreed, and as a result I became fast friends with the show's producer, Robert Liccata. Robert was impressed with my animal knowledge, and when a new show was in the planning stage, he gave me a call.

"So, Marc, this is Bob Liccata, and I have an offer for you."

I was intrigued.

"What kind of offer?"

"Actually, it's a screen test for a new show about pets on our Extra Help series on Channel One."

I agreed to take the screen test, and then I heard nothing for a couple of weeks. I figured they had found some kind of expert, like a veterinarian, and had forgotten about me. Then I got another call. Apparently, the vet they had chosen refused to take a drug test, and so they were back knocking at my door.

"Heck, I'll pee in as many bottles as you want."

So, there I was, ready to embark upon my own show on which I would answer people's questions about animals. After I stopped being excited, I switched to fear. What if nobody called in? What if I looked like an idiot in front of millions of people? I decided to ask all my friends to call in with questions to be sure there was no dead air. As it turned out, I didn't need to worry. I was inundated with calls.

At first, I had only a couple of dogs and cats with me, usually Barney and whatever cats seemed to be in the mood. Three nights a week, I found myself standing there in front of the camera for a whole hour, not knowing what to do with my arms or hands. So I figured that the more animals I could bring on the show, the more I would be able to use my body, instead of just standing there looking uncomfortable. After a while, I decided to bring on Harry and set him on a T perch behind me.

I'd pick him up, put him on my shoulder, and place him back on his perch. Then he'd fly onto my shoulder, and that's where he decided to stay. From that moment on, he's always been with me when I appear on television. He's my good-luck charm. Of course, he did develop the challenging habit of pulling off my eyeglasses. We had to solve that problem quickly because I also had an IFB ("interruptible fold back," which feeds back to talent via earphone and is interrupted by the producer with cues) unit in my ear, and he began pulling that out, too. Thank goodness, I always wear turtlenecks and we were able to hide the wiring inside the collar before I went on camera—and before Harry knew where the wiring was. The ear unit was taped in with flesh-colored tape so Harry couldn't pull it out. The makeup woman and I had quite a ritual before every show.

In the beginning episodes, I kept all of the animals separated. I worked behind a table that had only three wheels. It was always tipping, and I had to use my foot to keep it from going over entirely. It was all I could do to handle one animal, multiple questions, and a problematic table. Until one night . . .

It was winter, and the heat had gone off in the studio. To keep warm, all of us—an African Grey parrot, a rabbit, a cat, a puppy, and I—were all bundled up together. We looked like a big monkey ball of animals plus one human. After the show, we received faxes and calls from viewers who loved seeing all of the animals mixed up together. I realized that the more we combined different species, the more interesting it was for the viewers—and for me. At one point, I conducted a contest for viewers to guess how many animals were actually on the set. From hamsters and gerbils to big dogs and parrots, there were sixty. That's the most I've ever been able to handle at one time.

The show was successful and the producers renamed it *Petpourri*, then *Metro Pets*. Unfortunately, the show moved to a different studio an hour away. Now I had to be driven into the city with all my animals. This was a live show, so we had to set up everything beforehand. My little show was now a great deal of work, but people loved it, and I loved doing it.

Then came that fateful day in 1997 when I got a phone call at seven in the morning.

"Hi, Marc, this is Martha Stewart."

I was already familiar with her show, because in the previous year one of her assistants had asked if I would bring over a couple of chinchillas for a taping. As it turned out, Martha had seen several of my episodes and loved the display of animals cascading everywhere.

"Well, Marc, it was everything I could do not to call you at six in the morning after I had seen your show. I would really like you to appear on my television show."

Two weeks later, a van arrived at my store, and we loaded all of the animals for my first appearance on Martha's show *Living*. I was so nervous I forgot to take Harry. That's the only time I've ever performed without him.

The show went well, and Martha created my own show for me, called *Petkeeping*, which aired for five years on syndicated television. Martha was determined to keep me "live," so she created a radio show for me on her Sirius Satellite Radio channel. That program, *Ask the Pet Keeper,* is still running. Truth is, I love radio most of all. I can talk as much as I want to, there's no lack of people calling in, the people are all so nice and appreciative, and I don't have to worry about putting together sets or managing animals.

Still, Martha had new plans for me. In 2005, I started to appear on Martha's new live-television show, *The Martha Stewart Show,* as the "pet keeper." I had found more than a media connection. I had found a kindred spirit.

I became the guardian for Martha's favorite bird, Coral Ann, an exceptionally beautiful Moluccan cockatoo with that breed's signature salmon crest. All of her feathers are vanilla tinged with orange, much like that old-fashioned orange and vanilla ice cream. She and Martha connected immediately, and Martha still considers Coral Ann "her" bird, even though Coral Ann lives in my store. Martha knows she doesn't have enough time for a cockatoo. Coral Ann is comfortable with that arrangement.

Beauty aside, where talent is concerned, Coral Ann is exceptional. She's extremely dexterous with her claws and can tie an overhand knot. If you give her a piece of string or a leather lanyard, she will tie knot on top of knot, all the way around herself or the cage. She also likes to talk on the phone, and it annoys her if a human talks on the phone without involving her in the conversation. Anyone near her cage knows the consequence of getting too close to her beak while chatting with someone: many holes in many shirts.

When she's on Martha's show, she's always on Martha's shoulder. I try to make sure Harry is as far away as possible from the shoulder where Coral Ann is sitting. Memories of Harry's attacking Coral Ann are still vivid for Martha and me. Those feathers were pulled out, and of course Martha still has them. She also has all of Coral Ann's molted feathers that I collect for her. Coral Ann's feathery finery adorns Martha's dressing room.

Martha visits Coral Ann whenever she can. In order to get to her house in the Hamptons, she has to drive right past my store. On one occasion, she showed up with her chows: Paw Paw, Zu Zu, and Empress Wu. The dogs had a great time in the store getting treats, and Martha had a great time playing with Coral Ann. It was lunchtime, and as everyone now knows, I never eat lunch.

"Marc, let's have lunch. Where should we go?"

For Martha, I'll eat lunch.

One of my friends owns a family-style restaurant, and I thought he might be excited to have Martha Stewart dining in his establishment. What a boost that could be for his business. I had always found his food to be excellent, so, full of confidence, I escorted Martha to his place. It must have been an off day because the food was terrible. Fortunately, the owner wasn't there. I kept looking at Martha's face to gauge her reaction. Always the lady, she never betrayed a hint of dissatisfaction. We finished what we could and returned to the store, where she gave one more kiss to Coral Ann before she left.

A couple of days later, I went back into the restaurant, and the owner came rushing up to me.

"Oh, my goodness. Martha was here? I never take time off, and this one day. . . . Ah! Such luck! Did she like the food?"

By now, the entire staff was looking at me, and I remembered something Alba had taught me: "Always throw water on a fire, never gasoline."

"Martha said it was the best restaurant ever. It was just great. It was the most wonderful restaurant."

I felt bad not being able to tell him the truth, but it meant so much to him, and he looked happy. To this day, he tells customers, "Martha Stewart ate here and she loved it."

I am a faithful servant to those I care about. When it comes to Martha's Coral Ann, I am truly Martha's steward.

CHAPTER 30

Elmo and the Great
Goldfish Caper

Barbara Fight and Jocelyn Santos, producers for Martha's show, are also important people in my life. Connecting with Martha reconnected me with Barbara and introduced me to Jocelyn, who was not only an accomplished dog trainer but also a top producer with Martha. It was after meeting Jocelyn that I reconnected with Barbara. I had become part of a remarkable team.

Working with these three talented women has given me the opportunity to create what I consider to be the best pet-keeping segments on television. I have learned how to offer information that is complete and accurate in as few as six minutes, regardless of the topic or animal.

"Marc, we want you to do a segment on brushing a cat's teeth."

In six minutes, of course. Not a problem. Barbara is a master of pacing, directing me off-camera on exactly what to do and say. The segment always comes off seamlessly.

I start with a cat's skull, so that I can show where all of the cat's teeth are. A live cat isn't likely to be that cooperative. Then instead of just describing how to brush those teeth, I show the viewer how to acclimate the cat to the toothpaste. I show how to desensitize the cat's gums, and then how to properly brush each tooth. All in six minutes.

I've shown people how to teach their birds to eat fruits and vegetables, and I've worked with children to show them how to do the things I do. All in six minutes, with Harry on my shoulder and Coral Ann on Martha's. Eye candy added to the main course.

That's not to say that every segment is smooth sailing, or should I say, "gliding." During one segment I brought on a sugar glider, which is a small marsupial. It looks like a flying squirrel, but it's not part of that family; it's a type of possum. Sugar gliders are native to Indonesia, but they're bred in captivity and kept as pets in the United States. Cute as they are, they do have very sharp little claws on their front feet. Enter Martha, the perennial good sport.

In a moment of exuberance, the little possum flew toward her head, but missed. Instead, the glider landed right on her face and nearly scratched her cornea. A real trooper, Martha just laughed off the accidental attack. That happened early in my relationship with her, and it helped to quickly forge the bond that she and I share. Most people, especially celebrities, would have thrown a fit, but Martha took it in stride and went on with the show—and with me.

I also got to do segments with Martha's beloved chow chow Paw Paw. He is a remarkable dog, and I even dedicated my first book with Bowtie Press to him because he had accomplished so much in his lifetime. He participated in the Westminster Kennel Club Dog Show, he sired a few litters of puppies, and he was a television celebrity. When he and I were on the show together, I would pick him up, clunk him into a basket, put him in the middle of a bunch of puppies or kittens or bunnies or birds, whatever. It didn't matter. He would wag his tail with a genuinely happy look on his face, and smile. Yes, Paw Paw smiled. He was probably the most fulfilled and contented dog I've ever seen in my life. He died peacefully of old age in Martha's kitchen. A good place to end his life.

That is indeed one of the joys of working with Martha. I can share the stage with my own animals, with an excitable marsupial, with a beloved dog, with a cat in need of dental attention, or with a puppet.

Probably the most famous "pet" I ever worked with was Elmo, the renowned Muppet. When I was told that the Muppets would be on her show that day, I was hoping to work with Big Bird, but he was too big to fit in the studio. So it was Elmo and me. I had to come up with something natural, where I could share some kind of knowledge, and I came up with the idea of using goldfish. As most people know, Elmo has a little goldfish named Dorothy who lives in a little bowl on the Muppet set. Since my good friend Russell raises fancy goldfish called Ranchus, I decided to feature those.

As a pet keeper, certainly I know that keeping goldfish in little bowls is cruel. Full-grown, a goldfish is almost a foot long, and those tiny bowls just don't work. In fact, Russell, who is also a member of the American Goldfish Society, has written letters to Sesame Street protesting that it's wrong to give children the impression that goldfish are happy in bowls. It's easy to imagine how many "Dorothys" have lived and died in Elmo's fish bowl over the years.

Aha! This would be a perfect segment for me to do with Elmo. He and I can talk about how Dorothy shouldn't live in that little bowl, and then he and I can put together a fish tank with a filter where Dorothy can live happily ever after.

When we taped the segment, I took along Harry and Darwin, my African Grey parrot. Darwin is a real ham, and I knew he'd be a fun addition to the segment. I also discussed my concept with Elmo's puppeteer and voice actor, Kevin Clash, who actually used to work with Captain Kangaroo. He loved the idea, and he assured me that Elmo would follow my leads.

There we were: Elmo, Dorothy, a variety of other goldfish, and me. Dorothy was in her little bowl, and I explained to Elmo that she would be much happier in a tank. I also showed him the other goldfish—fantails, Black Moors, and Orandas—and explained how they had evolved through the domestication process. I put six of them in the new tank, along with Dorothy, and Elmo exclaimed how happy they all looked, swimming together in their new home.

"Oh, no." Elmo sighed. "Now my little bowl looks empty and sad."

Not a problem. I had also taken along a betta, better known as a Siamese fighting fish, which is also a labyrinth fish. This species has a special organ in its head called the labyrinth organ that allows it to breathe air. They evolved in Southeast Asia, where they were able to survive in tiny, oxygen-deprived puddles. So long as the water in their little bowls is changed regularly, and as long as the fish are kept warm enough, bettas do very well in that small space. The whole segment went swimmingly, and the crew even applauded when we were finished. When it aired, it was a longer segment than usual—nearly ten minutes long—and I was really pleased.

To my surprise, after the segment had aired, my producers brought me a huge stack of letters divided into three piles. The first pile was from goldfish enthusiasts, who I thought would be grateful for my sharing good information about bowls, but who instead nitpicked the way I had prepared the tank. "Too many goldfish." "Too much water into the tank, too fast." "Too much" this and "too much" that. It was very disheartening. Apparently, they forgot that this was a short piece about goldfish conducted with a puppet and two parrots, not an in-depth look at goldfish husbandry.

The second pile of letters was from people who keep their goldfish in little bowls. This group defended their habitats, insisting that their goldfish were alive and well after many years in confinement. One person even mentioned that she carried the little goldfish bowl with her from room to room, so that the fish wouldn't get lonely. That one, at least, was cute.

The third pile was from betta enthusiasts who felt that I had maligned their special fish by suggesting that bettas were somehow more disposable than standard goldfish.

By the time I got through the three piles, I was visibly upset. Martha noticed, and she offered such pithy advice that I still think of it today.

"Marc, do you think I make everybody happy? It's impossible to make everybody happy. But the people that I do make happy— and that you make happy—really appreciate what you and I do. Those are the people to focus on."

I smiled. It's no wonder that Martha has not only achieved great success in her life, but also has survived its rough bumps. She knows what matters, and who.

It was because of Martha and producer Jocelyn Santos that I was able to create one of my favorite programs. Jocelyn always makes me look good in my appearance and demeanor on camera. She was the one who came up with the idea of "Presidential Pets."

American presidents since George Washington have owned a surprising variety of pets, and she thought this would be an entertaining and informative show.

We started with presidential dogs, and we built a ramp that led up to a flat part where I would stand. My assistant stood at the left part of the ramp, and the dogs with their owners were all lined up at the beginning of the ramp. Jocelyn had been a successful dog trainer, and her expertise made everything go smoothly. She also had powerful connections with the Westminster Kennel Club Dog Show and knew host David Frei personally. Whatever dog breed we needed, we got it. We had George Washington's foxhound, Franklin Roosevelt's Scottish terrier, Richard Nixon's cocker spaniel, and a host of others.

Each dog would come up the ramp when called, then stop on the flat stage, and I would proceed to talk about the breed while I "stacked" it, showing off its best breed characteristics, and then telling one or more interesting stories about the president and his special dog. Then I would send the dog back down the ramp, and the next dog would be called. The audience loved it, and that encouraged us to produce more "pet" segments.

From dogs we moved on to other animals, like those owned by previous presidents. We featured John F. Kennedy's hamsters, canaries, and ponies; Abraham Lincoln's goats; and Teddy Roosevelt's hyacinth macaw, among many others. Remus played Teddy Roosevelt's parrot, one of the most famous pets we featured because of a sudden urge on my part. Remus was standing on a perch behind me, and something made me grab one of the little American flags on the platform and hand it to Remus. Not only did he grab the flag, he flew off the perch and landed on my shoulder, all the time holding the flag in his beak. I'm sure people thought I had trained him to do that. Now they know the truth.

Another funny segment involved St. Bernards. Instead of having only one dog that I would talk about and stack according to dog-handler standards, Jocelyn had brought me five adult dogs and a few puppies. There I was, sitting on a sofa with these dogs all over me, covered in drool and slobber. I loved it; I was having a ball. "Presidential Pets" was a television inspiration, and I owe it all to Jocelyn. I don't work with her on television anymore since Martha's show is now live; but we still work together on my satellite radio show. I wouldn't be half the presenter and educator I am today if it weren't for her.

She's got presidential style.

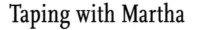

CHAPTER 31

Taping with Martha

People who see me on Martha's show might think that she and I do everything off the cuff. Nothing could be further from the truth.

In the early days, when the shows were taped, we had the luxury of editing material before it ever aired. Still, even then, doing retake after retake is expensive, and time on television is indeed money. So I had to write a script.

If I were going to do a segment on cockatiels or on house-training puppies, I would write out everything I planned to say and do. That also meant memorizing everything I wrote down, because I don't read the teleprompter when I'm on camera.

So today, after I've written my script, I e-mail it to the producer, who breaks it all down. She'll test it for timing and where to put all the props. Before the show, she'll get all those props ready.

When Martha is doing the segment with me, she doesn't read my script. She wants to be "in the moment" and truly learn from what I'm saying. That makes new shows even more challenging, because there's not much Martha doesn't know about animals, and I have to be creative in finding things she doesn't know about. One thing is for sure: our repartee always works.

For a live show, this is how my day goes: Because the show airs at eleven in the morning in New York, we tape it at ten. My typical segment is six minutes long, and everything has to be perfect, because we're doing this in front of a live audience. So at nine o'clock we rehearse for an hour. My day has started much earlier than that.

I arrive at my store at two in the morning. Everything I need—animals, carriers, cages, brushes, personal props—has to be ready when her production assistant, Kyle, arrives with the van at five. We have to leave by five-thirty in order to get to Manhattan by seven. It will take me another hour to do all of my personal adjustments to the set, and get all the animals situated after we arrive.

In 2008, our Easter segment about rabbits pushed everyone to their limits. I planned to take Harvey, my Flemish rabbit, and twenty other bunnies, along with Harry and Coral Ann and a host of rabbit props. And this wasn't one segment; it was two separated by a commercial break, so this one was going to involve extra preparation.

I had done the scripts and sent them on to my producer, Barbara Fight, and everything seemed fine. We were due to shoot the following Thursday, and I felt ready. I even invited my literary agent to join me on the show as my helper. She was ecstatic. An animal lover with her own menagerie, she started rearranging her schedule so that she could be there.

The day before the shoot, I arrived at the store at my usual "nontaping" time of five o'clock as I always do, and parked in the lot to enjoy my newspapers and coffee. Out of my rearview mirror, I noticed a van parked in front of the store. It was far enough away that I couldn't see who the driver was. I assumed it was a delivery of tropical fish, and that the driver was in his vehicle sleeping until I helped him unpack. I took a little more time than usual, and got out of the car around six-fifteen. Then as I was leisurely walking across the parking lot, I saw a frantic person jump out of the van and run toward me.

"Kyle, what are you doing here? We're shooting the segment tomorrow!"

Kyle didn't know what kind of car I drove, so he had no way of knowing that it was me sitting in the car all that time.

"No, there was a schedule change. I'm sure someone called you."

"It's all right. I must have missed the call."

Panic. It was now six-fifteen and we should have left more than an hour earlier.

Now I was the one who was frantic. Unlocking the door, we both rushed inside and quickly gathered up all the bunnies. If I'd had to collect a variety of different species, it would have been a catastrophe.

Somehow, I managed to get all the animals together, got them in the van, ran downstairs, got my good clothes out of the closet, ran upstairs, jumped in the van, and off we went. By then it was six-thirty and we were at the height of New York morning traffic.

At this point, Kyle was nearly hysterical because we were running late. No, not "nearly," he *was* hysterical. I had my own little hysterical thought. My literary agent, also the author of her own book about a parrot, had rearranged her entire schedule to accommodate coming with me to the show as my helper. Could she possibly change everything again, and make it down to the studio by eight?

At six-thirty I could only hope she was up. No such luck. By the time she got my message, it was nearly eight, and there was no way she'd be able to do it. Like me, she accepts random events as "the way it was meant to be," and she wasn't upset, just disappointed. I apologized, and now my attention turned back to my own minor hysteria.

There were two special Easter bunny segments. Not just one segment but two. The show couldn't cobble itself around a missing segment of this type and length. Traffic was unusually heavy, and it seemed we were hardly moving at all. Then a strange calm came over me while we sat on the Long Island Expressway, stuck in heavy traffic. This would be fine. I knew that everything would be okay.

I've talked to fishermen who reach that moment of lucidity when they just know that today will be the day they catch that big fish, or football players who just know that the ball in the air will land safely in their hands.

I relaxed. Miraculously, the traffic opened up like the Red Sea, and we pulled into the studio at seven-thirty. Everyone there was in a panic, grabbing carriers and props, but we managed to get everything inside and set up. The rehearsal went smoothly, and the segment itself was seamless. It was one of the best segments I ever did on Martha's show, and it still airs on YouTube.

It's funny how sometimes the worst possible scenario can turn into the best possible scenario in life, and sometimes the best scenario can turn into the most horrible. It just goes to show how random events take over our lives, and we really don't have any control over those random events. I've learned that not from people, but from animals.

Random doesn't apply when it comes to supershoots for

Martha's company. Supershoots run from nine in the morning until six in the evening. This means taping as many as thirteen segments, each ten minutes long. Each segment involves a different animal or animals, so everything we need has to come with me in the van, including food and cages to accommodate the animals' long waits to get their ten minutes of fame.

For me, it means not sleeping the night before. Not enough time. I'm writing scripts for the two days prior to shooting, and then I have to get all the animals ready the night before so we're ready when we're picked up at five the next morning. Arriving at the studio, we look like a somewhat organized caravan, with sounds and smells coming at us from everywhere.

At the end of the shoots, I'm absolutely drop-dead tired. My head hurts, and I just stand there, exhausted. It's not that I've done any heavy work; I didn't have to lift or carry anything. All I've done is talk to the camera, all day long. It takes me three days to recover from one of those all-day shoots.

Then I look at Martha, still going like an Energizer Bunny. Between her shoots, she's on the phone, reading e-mails, holding meetings, then back to the shoot at hand. After we finish taping at six, she's off to business meetings that can easily run until eleven.

I take a deep breath. If Martha can do it, so can I.

CHAPTER 32

When Lilacs Last Bloomed in Martha's Garden

Contrary to what many people might think, what most endears Martha to me is not the media exposure she's brought into my life, but our shared passion for every aspect of the natural world. Like Gerald Durrell, and like me, Martha is fascinated by every detail of her environment. If she and I happen to be walking anywhere in nature, and she hears a bird singing in a tree, she will stop and look up into the tree to find out what kind of bird it is. She has to be able to identify it. She also wants to know the name of every plant she sees, every rock she sees, every cloud formation, every body of water, absolutely everything around her. Unfortunately, she and I don't have many opportunities to simply walk about in nature; but when we do, it's clear that we are very much alike. In a way, she's a female version of me, and a sister to Alba Ballard. Even at home, her collection of animals and her garden amplify how much we are kindred spirits.

The first time I visited Martha's "wonderland" in Turkey Hill, Connecticut, she immediately pulled me in the direction of her chicken coops. As we passed the raspberry patch, all those beautiful vines trailing on carefully arched wires, she stopped to casually fix a few of the wires. She didn't place a call and have someone else do it for her. She knew just what the raspberries needed and fixed them.

When we arrived at the chicken coops, I could scarcely believe what I was seeing. All of the coops were neatly lined with gravel; there was no mud anywhere. On the outside of the coops, beautiful climbing roses trailed up the sides and across the tops. Inside the coops were several different breeds, all looking quite content to be "cooped up" in such comfortable surroundings. At one end of the chicken coops was a special area where all of the chickens were very old, many with their combs hanging down over their faces, looking like venerable, ancient birds.

"What are these chickens, Martha?"

Of the hundred or so chickens she had in the other coops, there had to be roughly thirty of these older birds.

"Oh, these are the chickens that are too old to lay eggs anymore."

"But what do they do there?" I'd never thought about retirement communities for chickens.

"Well, they just live out their lives there. They've laid eggs for me all these years. What else would I do with them? So I made this special coop for them."

How very sweet, I thought. She led me away from the chicken coops and back into the house. Inside, there were cats everywhere. At the time, I had no idea how many cats Martha had. Some of her most valuable furniture was covered with sheets so that the animals could lie wherever they wanted. When company came, she would take off the sheets. When she was by herself, this was cat country. In reality, she only had eight or so at her highest cat population; it only seemed like more because everywhere we went, they seemed to be there. Sitting at the kitchen table, a cat would jump up, and Martha would casually scratch the cat's neck while continuing the conversation. A dog or two would walk into the kitchen and she'd switch her attention to them, never breaking stride with what we were discussing. Everything was in flow, everything in synch.

As much as Martha travels, all of her animals have become happily socialized, at ease with whoever is in the house, including those whom Martha hires to take care of the animals when she's away. The animals are content whether or not she's home. They seem to understand her comings and goings, and none of them seems stressed by her schedule.

Her most surprising pets, at least for me, were the chinchillas. On one occasion, she called me up because one of her favorites, Snow White, was distressed.

"Marc, I know that Snow White doesn't feel well. I saw that she urinated in a corner of the cage where she normally never urinates. There must be something wrong, and I thought maybe you could come and take a look."

Over I went, after I was finished at the pet store; and sure enough, Snow White appeared sick. Between Martha's special "animal gene" and mine, we figured out that the problem was with her food, and we corrected it.

In the background, I could hear the canaries singing inside their grand cages. Certainly, the Chinese are masters of carving these specially crafted cages for their prized birds, and Martha was indeed a master of her own bird cages. Those sweet bird notes were coming from very happy canaries.

"Now that you're here, I also wanted to talk to you about a special segment for the holidays."

Christmas is one of Martha's favorite holiday events, and this year she had an especially ambitious idea.

"I want to recreate the 'Twelve Days of Christmas' for my Christmas special."

"You mean, like 'swans a' swimming' and other big, unmanageable animals?"

We both laughed.

"I'm sure I can abbreviate it a little bit." My mind began to put together this animal tableau. When the segment finally aired, we had made some creative modifications to the original script.

Instead of the partridge sitting in a pear tree, the partridge sat in Martha's lap.

"They're ground birds, Martha. It will never perch in a tree." Instead, I put Odo, a kookabura, in the pear tree. It's a type of kingfisher from Australia, and it makes an interesting laughing noise. Odo was very well trained and could make that laughing sound whenever I asked him to.

Joining him were the two turtledoves, and three Japanese silky chickens instead of the French hens, which are also known as Mille Fleur. Unlike their "thousand flower" name, the Mille Fleur are very plain brown birds; so I took poetic license in choosing the Japanese breed with their fluffy feathers and little pom-pom on top of their heads. All in a dither, Martha knew the difference.

"Those aren't French hens; they're Japanese. They're Japanese."

"No one's going to know. Even if they do, no one will care."

"What about the calling birds. Will we have those?"

"Martha, there's no such thing as a calling bird. Well, not as a breed, anyway. They're assorted finches native to Europe."

The reason they had been given the name "calling birds" was

because Europeans used to take a male finch, put him in his cage, and place the cage in the middle of a field. The finch would call out, and another male finch would fly down to check out the intruder. When he saw the cage, he would land next to it in order to check out the caged bird, only to be caught in the trap that had been set down into the grasses.

I had decided to use canaries instead, because they're from the same genus and sound like finches.

"I'm going to use red canaries, which I'll train to fly and land on the Christmas wreath. They'll make great little calling birds."

Martha was so enthralled with my trained canaries, she took the two pairs home after the show.

On another occasion when I visited Martha at her new home in Bedford, New York, I was once again reminded of how much she and I think alike.

I had been invited to a dinner party with several of Martha's other friends, and as always, the meal was a gourmet delight. After dinner, while her other guests were visiting in the living room, she and I went into the kitchen to wash dishes. Yes, Martha does wash dishes.

In the kitchen was a beautiful one-piece soapstone sink. It was about six feet long and about eight inches deep. It had three drains and three faucets. She put the dishes into the sink, spread them out evenly beneath the three faucets, and the dishes were done in what seemed like seconds. Obviously, she had designed the sink herself.

I stood there watching her and only one word came to mind: turtles.

I began muttering to myself how perfect this sink would be

for turtles, with three faucets, well-spaced drains, and proper depth. Baby turtles are especially dirty and it's very hard to keep their habitats clean. This was ideal!

"What are you mumbling about?"

Martha wasn't being peevish; she was simply curious.

"I was just thinking that this would be the perfect sink for keeping baby turtles."

Martha was right there "in the sink" with me.

"You know, I never quite thought of it that way before; and I probably wouldn't have thought of it that way without your being here. What a clever idea."

That's the Martha most people could never imagine. Most of my favorite memories of Martha and me don't really have anything to do with business. Many of those moments have also occurred when I least expected them.

My wife's favorite flowers are lilacs, especially the purple ones. It was a perfect spring day, and lilacs were in bloom everywhere, both white and purple. It was also my wife's birthday, and Martha and I were just finishing a shoot. Seeing all those lilacs on the set reminded me that I needed to pick up some flowers for Kathi.

"Oh, that's right. Today is my wife's birthday. She just loves lilacs; they're her favorite flowers. Unfortunately, she likes the purple ones; we only have white ones at home."

I said it offhandedly, and went about the business of gathering up all of my animals and getting them crated up to go back home. Her production assistant was waiting patiently for me in the van, and finally I was ready to go.

There on the front seat was a huge vase full of purple lilacs, with a lovely card that said, HAPPY BIRTHDAY TO KATHI.

I was stunned. What a thoughtful thing to do.

Another time I had gone to Martha's house to discuss a new segment, and the sight of an enormous patch of prickly pear cactus struck me. It was the middle of the day and the cacti were in bloom. It was breathtaking.

"Oh, jeez, these cacti are beautiful! I would love to have a patch like that."

That's all I said, and no more was said about it. About a month later, I received a package from Martha. Inside were thirty little "cactuslings." I was shocked. After I had admired her splendid cactus patch, she had rooted these for me, and then mailed them to me when they were ready. She didn't hire someone to do it for her. She prepared them with her own hands.

I planted them in front of my house, and to this day I still have the Martha Stewart Cactus Patch.

Martha hasn't just given or sent me thoughtful gifts; sometimes I'm the gift—to herself—especially when it comes to searching for new, interesting antiques.

For the record, I hate antiquing. When I was a child, my parents would drag me hither and yon in search of special collectibles. We lived in a big Victorian house, and it was filled with the results of seemingly endless trips to dark, dusty stores. I hated the way those stores smelled, the mustiness, and the way the floorboards always seemed to creak eerily. I hated the kinds of people who owned the stores, looking smug and bored at the same time. I hated standing around while my parents "oohed" and "aahed" over some little piece of china, and I swore that I would never do that when I grew up.

Enter Martha.

She and I were doing a shoot near her home in Connecticut when she got a call that we had to go back to her studio, which was about a ten-minute drive from her home. Because we both had to go, she offered to drive.

We get into her car and off we go. All of a sudden she makes a sharp right turn down off the main road, and I think to myself, "Where are we going? Maybe she knows a shortcut to the studio."

No such luck.

We pulled into a parking lot in front of an antique store.

"You've got to come with me. I want you to see what wonderful things they have."

To myself I'm thinking, *I can't believe this is happening.*

So, I follow her inside, the door creaking as we walk through. The boards under my feet are creaking, and there's that familiar musty smell.

Dutifully, I follow her up and down the rows of "wonderful things." Whenever she finds something she likes, she hands it to me, and soon my arms are full of dirty, musty "wonderful things." I can't believe this is happening to me. When my arms are so full that I can't possibly hold any more, we make our way to the cash register, pay for the booty, and back we go to the car. As we continue on our drive to the studio, I have to laugh. Not out loud. Martha is expressing how delighted she is at our finds, and how much fun it was to go there with me. All I'm thinking is that my parents are going to be amazed when they hear that I went antiquing with anyone, especially Martha Stewart. Oh, God, will there be other times?

Fortunately, given both of our schedules, that was the only time.

What I cherish, perhaps most of all, are the times Martha cooks for me. Everyone knows she loves to cook. She also loves to cook for me, whipping up something in a flash and enjoying the fact that I enjoy what she fixes. In those moments, I'm back in Alba Ballard's kitchen, being regaled with sweet stories, new information about animals, and the shared camaraderie of our animal passion. I am so blessed.

CHAPTER 33

From Dancing with the Stars
to Standing with the Losers

Sometimes those blessings are mixed, like the time I accepted Martha's invitation to a special fund-raising gala. When I'm not in my pet store, appearing on television, or off on some antiquing adventure with Martha, I've also attended many media events with her. I've sat next to her at the Emmys, all decked out in formal attire instead of my signature turtleneck, and participated in all manner of other balls, ceremonies, and formal events. Under her careful training—Martha is my best teacher—I've learned how to look and feel comfortable in these upscale surroundings. The most memorable, though, has to be the animal welfare fundraiser to which Martha had invited me as her guest.

The invitation came at a really low point in my financial life, and I had no idea where I was going to find the money to rent a tuxedo. Fortunately, the owner of the tuxedo store in Rockville Centre, Long Island, wanted a cockatiel for his son, so I traded him the bird he wanted in exchange for the tuxedo. Now, at least, I looked good. The second challenge would be parking. The hotel on Fifth Avenue was right next to Central Park, and parking could easily cost fifty dollars or more, money I didn't have. Again, by chance, one of my special customers lived in an elegant town house about fifteen blocks away from the hotel. He had his own driveway and garage, and he told me I could park in his driveway. Now I just had to walk the fifteen blocks to the hotel. I reached into my pocket for the invitation that had the name of the hotel and it wasn't there. There were several hotels up and down Fifth Avenue, and I didn't know which one I was going to. Three times I walked right past it. Again, chance intervened, and I literally bumped into my producer, Jocelyn Santos, who was on her way to the event as an invited guest.

"Thank God I bumped into you. I can't find my invitation and I don't remember the name of the hotel."

"Not a problem, Marc. We're here."

If Jocelyn hadn't bumped into me, I might have wandered around New York for days.

So we get inside, are seated at Martha's table, and the event gets under way. I'm sitting next to Martha's daughter, Alexis, and having a great conversation with her in between the speeches and the applause. Martha gives a speech, too, and it's clear that the audience really loves her. After the speeches and the dinner are over, it's time to socialize—not one of my strong suits, but Martha's tutelage helps boost my confidence. Besides, I recognize some of the people milling about; they're long-time customers at my store, so I'm feeling more relaxed. One of those customers walks over to our table and introduces a very attractive young woman.

"Mr. Morrone, I told this young lady that you were probably the only person in this room who would know who her great-grandfather was."

Following his lead, and feeling increasingly self-assured, I quipped back.

"Well, let me try. Who is your great-grandfather?"

I immediately recognized the last name, and I responded that I knew quite well the stories about her relative, who was a world-class explorer who had traveled to many continents and discovered many types of animals.

"Some of those animals even bear your great-grandfather's last name."

"Oh, Mr. Morrone, you're so intelligent. Will you dance with me?"

"Well, okay, sure." I really wasn't all that sure. I'm a very shy guy, but she was so lovely in her emerald-toned gown and her beautiful yellow hair. Her name was Daphne.

We start dancing, and I'm beginning to feel a little like a male version of Cinderella in my rented tuxedo and remotely parked carriage, dancing with this rather enchanting young woman.

"So, Daphne, what do you do for a living?"

"We're philanthropists."

I'm not surprised. Many of the people at this event devote their lives to helping worthy causes, especially animals. I respect what they do.

"And what do you do, Mr. Morrone?"

Here I am, at this financial low point, and I search for the right thing to say.

"Well, I'm the head of a nonprofit organization." It wasn't a lie. My pet store hadn't turned a profit in five years.

"That's so nice. I have a lot of respect for people who run those kinds of foundations."

"Well, thank you, Daphne. I'm glad you think so."

While enjoying my time on the dance floor, I notice that it's ten o'clock. I have to get back to LaGuardia Airport and pick up an incoming shipment of birds by eleven. My dance card had expired.

"I'm so sorry, Daphne, but I have to go. I can't tell you where I'm going, but I need to go now."

As I rush toward the exit, I notice from the corner of my eye that Daphne is waving her handkerchief in my direction, waving good-bye. To this day, I can't imagine where she had been keeping that handkerchief, given that her gown was strapless.

I wave good-bye back to her, feeling even more like Cinderella fleeing the ball when I realize that I don't know what elevator to use, and I'm forced to run down seemingly endless flights of stairs to reach the street.

I bolt through the door, trying to adjust my focus toward the task at hand. I run the fifteen blocks to my car, jump in, and head toward the airport. My head is filled with images of my dancing with Daphne to lovely classical music among all of the glitterati. Those images quickly disappear when I arrive at the terminal at exactly eleven o'clock, just in time to meet my birds.

There I stand in my rented tuxedo, looking very out of place in front of the surly agent who's sitting at his desk reading the newspaper and chewing gum. I'm back in my real life.

"Excuse me, sir."

His head doesn't move.

"Excuse me, sir. I'm here to pick up some birds."

With that, he grudgingly raises his eyes and glares at me across his newspaper. I know he's staring at my formal attire and thinking that I must be thinking I'm someone special. I'm back with the wicked stepmother.

"You think, think, you're somethin', somethin', special 'cause you're wearin', wearin' a tuxedo? Well, you're not. Go stand over there, there, in line with the rest of the losers."

So I walk over to the wall and lean against it, sandwiched in with all the other unhappy people who need something in the middle of the night. I ruminate on the previous few hours at an elegant ball, dancing with a beautiful woman, and sharing the festivities with Martha Stewart and other luminaries. Here I am, back in line with the rest of the "losers."

Eventually, I claim my shipment of birds and head back to the pet store, where I clean and feed them. I'm the pet keeper and I'm a very happy man, and certainly not a loser.

CHAPTER 34

The Baby Bird Heist

August 2007 was not a happy time in my life. In fact, it was a profoundly low point in my pet-keeping career.

I arrived at the store as usual, parked in my usual spot, and leisurely enjoyed my coffee and newspapers. In the middle of my quiet time, the butcher from down the street came up to my car and knocked on the window.

"Hey, Marc, somebody broke your window last night."

I got out of the car and he continued.

"It must have been those animals at the bar."

There are two bars just down the street from my store, and it's not unusual for a rowdy bunch to hang around the parking lot until four in the morning. I would frequently arrive later in the morning to find beer bottles and garbage all over.

"I bet it was them who kicked in the glass."

I couldn't believe it.

"No way. That glass is half-inch-thick plate glass. You can't kick it in."

Sure enough, the butcher was right. The glass was all broken in, but in such a way that it didn't set off the electric eye that would have set off the alarm.

I went inside and looked around. It took a while for me to figure out what was going on.

I walked in another twenty feet and got to the upstairs bird room. The cash registers hadn't been touched. Good news so far.

There are two entrances to the bird room, one that's behind the counter and always open, and the public entrance that is made of glass and is also unlocked. Apparently, the thieves didn't know that, because there was glass all over the floor. They had broken the glass to get into the room, not knowing that all they had to do was open the door and walk in.

Whoever had described the layout to the person or persons who broke in wasn't aware of how easy it was to get into the bird room from either of those entrances.

During the day, the birds are loose on top of their cages. At night, we put them all in sleeping cages. My inventory at that time was very high. It was August, and typically a good selling month in my store. Each sleeping cage had twenty birds in it: blue-fronted Amazons, African Greys, cockatoos, and other assorted parrots. The thieves grabbed all of the cages and just pushed them through the hole in the door, took them to their vehicle, and were gone. The spaces where the cages had been sitting looked like gaping wounds.

The police arrived quickly, followed by the press. The Associated Press had the story out in no time, to newspapers all over the world. At eight in the morning, Martha called. She'd already heard about the robbery and wanted to make sure I was all right. Over the next week reporters and camera people were in my store day after day. It was agony retelling what had happened. I'm the kind of person who doesn't like to talk about it when something bad happens to me. I don't make an issue out of it. I just bury it inside a little chest in my heart, close the chest, and lock it with a key. Rehashing the event over and over again was excruciating.

During that week I rebuilt all the cages that had been stolen. The sight of their empty spaces made me weep. It was so horrible. I couldn't believe that someone would be so envious of me that they would do such a thing. I also couldn't believe that nobody had seen the robbery taking place. The bar closed at four and I was there by five. Whoever planned this had to have known when I would arrive and had carefully worked out all the details.

My birds never came home to me, despite the hard efforts of the police. My speculation is that the thieves cut off the birds' identification bands and sold the birds at swap meets and flea markets. Financially, the loss was devastating, and I'm still recovering from it years later.

Two weeks after the robbery, I was scheduled to appear on Martha's show. I was determined to keep my commitments, and so I did the show. When she asked me on the air about what had happened, I started to weep. I apologized for my tears, and Martha was quick to assure me that those tears needed no apology. Ironically, one woman who saw the program was so moved by what happened that she called me up later that day. She had just sold her memoir about a parrot that died and asked if she could send me an advance reading copy; she said it might help with the grief. I told her to send the book, and that started the relationship that led to this memoir.

The grief is still there for me. When you raise baby birds, each one has a little quirk or characteristic that makes that bird a special individual. This one likes that food, and that one doesn't. This one likes to be touched, that one doesn't. There was a blue-fronted Amazon who had a peculiar way of eating, and an African Grey that liked its head touched in a certain way. Those are still vivid images. I especially remember the Amazon because unlike most blue-fronts, who have an equal amount of blue and yellow on their heads, this bird had no yellow, and he was so difficult to feed that I constantly worried whether or not he would grow up to be a strong bird. At the time he was stolen, he was well on his way to becoming a big, healthy bird, all because of the attention I had given him.

Wherever my birds are, maybe some of those owners will read this book and at least understand how I feel. I don't expect anyone to call me up, but it would be comforting to know that at least a few of those birds are safe and content.

Thinking back to the "hyacinth heist" when my business was just getting started, that theft didn't have the same feel of treachery that this one did. Those thieves seemed more "in the moment," seizing an opportunity without any particular malice. The thieves who stole my baby birds were cruel and calculating and acted in cold blood.

Time to put the lock back on that little chest inside my heart.

PART V

ANIMALS IN THE SPOTLIGHT

CHAPTER 35

A Dancing Raven Performs
at Lincoln Center

My other calling, if I weren't the pet keeper, would be animal trainer. If I were an animal trainer, I would spend all of my time with my favorite animals and earn my living by doing so. In order for me to become a trainer like Ray Berwick or Frank Inn or Rudd Weatherwax, I would have to own a very large stock of animals with which I could work. Even though I'm not a trainer like those men, I have had considerable experience working with animals in a number of performance environments.

Like Ray Berwick, I thoroughly enjoy crows and ravens; and my raven, Dante, has an impressive résumé of roles in still ads, television commercials, and even a role in the Metropolitan Opera. Four years ago, the producer of an elaborate opera being imported from Japan contacted me in search of a raven that could perform in one wild, weird dance segment with the dancer. The dancer would execute his exuberant, jerky moves while the raven followed him around on the ground, somehow staying in "rhythm" with the dancer's erratic movements. Then when the dancer stopped, the raven would fly up to a perch, and the dancer would pick up the raven and walk offstage with it. I reviewed the video of the opera and thought to myself, *Dante can do this.*

There in my store, I became the wild Japanese dancer, practicing with Dante until he got all the moves and timing right. When it was show time, we headed to Lincoln Center, where Dante gave the performance of a lifetime. Later, the producer said that of all the ravens who had appeared in this opera all over the world, Dante was the best. I was proud; Dante looked prouder.

I've also been fortunate enough to work with some famous actors as a performance trainer. One such production was the movie *The Survivors*, starring Walter Matthau and Robin Williams. At the time, Robin had a double yellow-headed Amazon, so he understood a little more about parrots than most. The producers needed a hyacinth macaw, and Remus was perfect for the part. In what may be the movie's most famous scene, Robin walks into his boss's office and his boss isn't there. Suddenly, a large parrot climbs up onto the boss's chair and tells Williams that he's fired.

The scene began, Robin walked in, and I was hiding behind the chair with Remus. I put some peanut butter in his mouth (parrots love peanut butter; and no, it doesn't stick to the roof of their mouth) and then lifted him up so that his beak hooked over the top of the chair. Of course, he pulled himself up, and because he had peanut butter in his mouth, he started to move his beak up and down in order to eat the peanut butter. Robin's a consummate actor, and he just pretended that the parrot was giving him the ax and responded accordingly. Later on, words were dubbed "into the mouth of the parrot," and the scene was a smashing success. Applause, please, for Remus.

I also have what may be the most popular bat in New York for photographic and film shoots. In addition to my bat, I've provided reptiles and other assorted species to any number of movie and still shoots.

With television, what I have done and still do is diverse. I choose not to be one of those animal people, "experts," who go from show to show, trotting out their little menageries for the world of television viewers. Their animals are socialized, not trained, and while the setup is that the viewers are being educated, it's really all about entertainment—usually at the expense of the animal handler. Whether it's a chimp jumping on Johnny Carson's chest or a python wrapping itself around Ellen DeGeneres's leg, the purpose of the animal's presence is to make the audience laugh and the animal handler wince. In contrast, I love what I do on *The Martha Stewart Show,* because Martha genuinely cares about informing her audience. She and I are a great team, and we share very similar values about animals and animal care.

CHAPTER 36

Behind the Scenes with Animal Trainers

Ever since I was a child and first saw animals "acting" in movies, performing animals have always intrigued me. I've always admired people who have performing animals. When done right, those performances are some of the best entertainment available.

For the everyday person, entertainment might be having a dog that can walk off leash. The owner takes his dog out to the park, and other dog owners admire the fact that his dog is so well trained that he doesn't have to be "tied" to the owner. The owner gets praise, the dog gets praise, and the dog begins to figure out that walking leash-free has two benefits. He doesn't have to be tugged and pulled away from all the good places he wants to sniff, and he gets positive attention not only from his owner but also from complete strangers. That is the essence of a happy performing animal.

If I had the time, which unfortunately I don't, I would love to teach animals to perform on television and in movies. Some of my biggest "heroes" are animal trainers. Hopefully, all the advances in computer generation won't eliminate the need for live animals in the media.

In older movies, like those made in the 1950s and '60s, the

animals truly interacted with the human actors. Those animals genuinely enjoyed the spotlight. One of my favorites was the original version of *The Incredible Journey*. In one scene an old bull terrier is too weak to walk and is lying prostrate in a little clearing in the forest. Out of the forest come two little bear cubs who go right up to the dog and start to annoy him. The dog barks furiously at the cubs, and lo and behold, the mother bear comes out of the woods and stands up on her hind legs, in a menacing pose. What's interesting about the bear's standing up on its back legs is that it's a trick. A bear that is going to hunt or attack stays on all fours like a wolf or a mountain lion. A bear in the air is a bear at risk, because its chest and abdomen are exposed. In real life, an attacking bear will be on all fours with its head low and jaws wide open. The only time two bears might go up on their hind legs is if they're males about to do battle. The idea is for one bear to show the other bear that he's bigger than the other one. The "smaller" bear will back off and run away, and the "bigger" bear will go right back down on all fours. If both males are the same size, they will fight on all fours.

In the movie scene, the bear is up on her hind legs, advancing toward the helpless dog, when who should appear but Tao, the famous Siamese cat. Fearless, he fluffs up his fur, yowling at the bear. Now enter the bull terrier's other companion, a Labrador retriever, who joins the cat and barks at the bear. When the bear sees both the dog and the cat harassing it, she drops down on all fours, retrieves her cubs, and goes back into the forest. How did the trainers do all that?

First, the bull terrier was easy. He was simply trained to lie down and stay there. The bear cubs came tumbling out of the forest and did what little bear cubs would normally do, be curious;

they began to explore the clearing, which included the dog. Getting the mother bear to stand up on her hind legs was the big trick. To accomplish that, the trainer tied a piece of string to the bear's back leg and let it out all the way behind her. Then the trainer stood up facing the bear, off camera. At the other end of the string was the trainer's daughter, whom the bear also knew. Now the trainer called the bear. The bear came out of the forest and walked right up to the dog, because she was totally familiar with dogs. Then the trainer raised his hands, which was the signal for the bear to stand up. The bear obeyed. Now came the cat, who behaved just the way a Siamese cat would, all puffed up and hissing. The Labrador retriever had been trained to bark on command, so that wasn't an issue at all. Next, the bear trainer lowered his hands, and the bear went back down on all fours. Finally, the trainer's daughter tugged on the string, reminding the bear to turn around and walk off the set, where it would be rewarded with marshmallows. Real animals and real actors require genuine talent and expertise on the part of the trainer.

Today, the bear would be filmed against a green screen, the cat against another screen, one dog against another screen, and then the whole thing would be choreographed using camera technology.

Another great "oldie" in which the scene was played out with real animals was an episode of *Lassie*. Trained by one of the greats, Rudd Weatherwax, all of the Lassies were first-class actors. In this particular scene, Lassie is walking through the forest and comes upon a field with sheep grazing in it. She sees a lamb that is obviously lost, and the lamb notices her in return. The lamb seems to think that Lassie is its mother and starts to follow her, while Lassie tries to get away from it. Then comes the big, bad wolf. Lassie runs at the wolf, and the two of them fight until the vanquished wolf finally runs away. Now Lassie feels some compassion for the lamb and begins to lick her. Together, they take off in search of the lamb's mother. Aha! They find a deer with a fawn. Maybe that's the lamb's mother. No, the deer kicks the lamb away, and the journey continues. Finally, they find the lamb's mother, and Lassie wanders off, only to find a second lost lamb. Another journey begins. Lassie finds that lamb's mother, and then she sits down, looking exhausted. She points her nose up into the air and howls. But no. Yet another lost lamb shows up, and off the two go in search of a third mother in one day. Lassie licks at the lost lamb, and the scene ends. Real animal actors, and real animal training. These trainers understand how the animal's mind works, and they have an innate sense of what the animal will respond to. Much like a human gymnastics coach, the best animal trainers can create amazing performances.

Benji is probably one of the best-known trained dogs in more modern movies. He was trained by Frank Inn, who also trained all the animals in *The Beverly Hillbillies* and *Petticoat Junction*. For Benji, Frank carried a bag of steak cubes whenever Benji was performing. Frank knew before it ever became popular that positive reinforcement works.

Ray Berwick was among the most masterful of trainers who trained numerous species, but he is probably best known for his birds. My personal favorite was Lala, the cockatoo who starred in the television series *Baretta*. That bird was nothing less than amazing. He could drink out of a bottle; he could pick up the telephone and answer it; he did all kinds of tricks. One of Ray's best-known films was *The Birds*. Except for the scene in which the crows are on the children's backs, all the scenes used real crows and seagulls that Ray had trained. Everything was staged and blocked; it couldn't happen the way it happened in the movie. For example, in one scene Tippi was standing in place and Ray tossed a bird at her, and the bird had been trained to fly to her shoulder. But Tippi was instructed to wave her arms in the air and scream, as if she were trying to bat the bird away. It's a very effective scene that nearly wiped her out, and it took almost a week to film.

One of the most famous scenes, very eerie, is the one in the playground in which the crows arrive one by one to land on the jungle gym. Ray had trained each crow to fly and land, one at a time, until the jungle gym was covered in crows. Then with one command, he called them all back. Even today, I marvel at what he accomplished in that movie.

A third well-known film for Ray was *The Birdman of Alcatraz*. Aside from the fact that the first canary egg Stroud discovers is actually a parakeet egg, not a canary egg, the rest of the film is absolutely authentic. I've read all of Robert Stroud's books, and he was a genius, especially when it came to his medications that he concocted long before the age of antibiotics. It was he who discovered that drafts blowing on birds could cause their kidneys to shut down. Stroud in real life was not at all a kind, compassionate man, but he was brilliant when it came to birds.

A more contemporary and much more upbeat, film, *Polly*, is nothing less than a celebration of birds having a great time as actors. Real actors, real scenes.

Not all performing animals are sweet dogs and agreeable birds. There are others who demand a much different approach to animal training.

CHAPTER 37

Beware the Chimpanzee with a Toothbrush in His Hand

E ven though there is nothing more entertaining than watching a performing chimp in movies or on television, I am personally not a fan of seeing them in these scenarios. Unfortunately, there's always an element of cruelty, because it's very difficult to work with chimps in a live situation. Chimps don't respond as well as other animals do to positive reinforcement, because no amount of reward can overwhelm the reality that in the wild they're constantly fighting with one another. A trainer never knows what will set a chimp off, or when. They're a lot like my family. One minute, they're hugging and kissing one another; the next minute they have nothing nice to say to one another. And the next minute, someone's saying, "What do you want for lunch?" With a chimp, the human could be on the menu.

Chimps are like my family except for the fact that they're much stronger than we are, and they hit one another all the time. If one chimp bops another chimp on the head, the chimp who has been hit just rubs his head and moves on to whatever's next. If a chimp bops a human being on the head, the head comes off. Maybe not literally, but a chimp blow is a serious one. Chimps also bite one another. The equivalent of "ouch!" and the bitten chimp is on its way. For a human, the result could be major disfigurement or death.

To help keep the human actors safe, many performing chimps have their teeth removed when they're still babies. Sometimes, this is obvious when we see a chimp open his mouth wide to "laugh" during a scene. If one looks closely, the missing teeth are obvious.

Once a chimp gets to be about five years old, his acting career is effectively over. He's too large, too strong, and too dangerous. I know several people who bought chimps as babies so that they could be used in television commercials, only to be stuck with that chimp for the rest of its life, easily forty to forty-five years. These owners had to build special enclosures, whose standards are dictated by the USDA, and where the chimp must be carefully maintained for years and years to come. Unless the owner can hire—indeed, find—an animal sitter, he or she is now a slave to the retired actor.

My favorite chimp movie is still *Project X* with Matthew Broderick. As far as a story goes, it's brilliant. Although the message of the movie is to reduce the use of animals in laboratories, many of those chimps in the movie were routinely punished in order to make them perform.

The gist of the movie was that chimps would be trained to use on flight simulators. Then the scientists would expose the chimps to lethal doses of radiation to determine how long the chimp could operate the simulator before it died of radiation poisoning. The justification for the experiments was that we needed to know those limits in case we had to go in and bomb Russia, a literal suicide mission for the pilot. Ultimately, the experiments fail because the chimps had no way of knowing that they were going to die at the end of the experiment, where humans would have figured this out.

Another "movie with a message" that impressed many people was *The Bear*, which was done without any cruelty. The bear actor, Bart, is very well known, but ironically in this movie most of the scenes were staged, and as was the case in *The Incredible Journey*, they are an example of superior filmmaking. An example of terrible filmmaking, in which the animals really did physically engage one another, is the much-loved movie *The Yearling*, with Gregory Peck. In that movie, the most dramatic scene in which the bear-hunting hounds attack a bear is an example of shortcuts and no animal training at all. The poor bear was muzzled—you can actually see the muzzle if you look closely—and he had been declawed. Then the director goaded the dogs to attack the bear. Those dogs are really biting the bear, and the poor bear can't bite back, because it's muzzled. It was horrific. A good animal trainer could have produced that scene, and none of the animals would have been hurt, but the director of that movie chose shortcuts to save money and time.

I realize that some people think it's abuse to make a horse fall down. The truth is, horses can be trained to do just about anything. Back in the 1940s there was a horse named Bess who is probably best remembered for her role in a World War Two movie in which a Japanese soldier shot her owner and he couldn't get up. The horse walked over to her owner, lay down beside him, and turned on her side so that the owner could grab her mane and pull himself over on her body. Then she stood up, and the man was able to right himself on her back. There was no bridle or reins; it was all about the horse's movements that she had been trained to do.

Blazing Saddles is another example of excellent horse training. Once the horse knows that nothing bad will happen to it, falling down isn't difficult at all. Horses in the wild fall down all the time; it's just that most people never see that, and so they think that a horse falling down is dangerous and cruel. It's not. And in *Blazing Saddles,* no one actually punches a horse. That's all trick photography.

The best animal movies are those in which the animals really act. Watching those movies reminds me that the relationship between humans and animals can even produce great drama. It becomes a creative partnership. That's an animal equation I love.

CHAPTER 38

The Zoo Puzzle:
Where Have All the Tigers Gone?

There are, of course, animals who never belong in our homes, animals we visit in zoos.

My first zoo experience was at the Bronx Zoo with my grandfather, Pietro. I was four years old and already collecting bugs to observe and study. "Lions and tigers and bears, oh, my!" was very different from little crawly things living in jars in my bedroom. The cages seemed big, the animals even bigger. I could smell them, hear them, and in some small way be in their world. I know that something profound must have happened to me among all those cages and noisy animals. By the time I was fifteen, the word *zoo* wasn't just part of my vocabulary; it was the driving force behind my passion for animals. I had learned from the work of Gerald Durrell that zoos were the best way to observe animals and gain knowledge about them. I never knew if there would be a real zoo in my future, but it was a dream I wasn't willing to relinquish. All these years later, and as the owner of one of the largest pet stores in the world—Parrots of the World—I still hold the dream of a zoo close to my heart.

For most people today, a zoo is a place you go to see animals and be entertained. Zoo owners in the past saw a way to breed animals in captivity while they earned money from those who came to see familiar and exotic species. In years past, zoos were primarily animal warehouses. The cages were relatively small, food was adequate but not optimal, and animal care was mostly "laissez-faire." The present status of most zoos is quite different from that of the past.

The breeding of wild animals in captivity has reached a tipping point. So many species have been replicated over and over again, that it's now only the most exotic that get any attention at all from the viewing public. Furthermore, zoos are no longer interested in exchanging animals among themselves, and so we have more animals than zoos can accommodate. Twenty or thirty years ago, if one zoo bred a tiger or a gorilla, there would always be another zoo that wanted one of those. Now, the majority of zoos have all the animals they need, so much of the breeding activity has stopped. Very few babies are seen at most zoos for that reason.

Many zoos today are doing an excellent job with their exhibits. The Bronx Zoo, for one, has a very clever tiger exhibit. They have a total of eight tigers, and the zookeepers let them into the viewing area in rotation, one at a time. From the tiger's perspective, he's entering that area for the first time, because he realizes immediately that another tiger was in there just before him. That means the tiger has to walk around and mark everything that was marked by the previous tiger, and personalize it. The tiger doesn't just lie there and sleep; he has to reestablish territory. The zoo visitor is thus guaranteed the experience of a tiger viewing.

The gorilla exhibit is also extraordinary. In one part of the exhibit, there is only one piece of glass separating the gorilla from the viewer. The viewer can lean his or her body up against the glass, and so can the gorilla. It's mesmerizing to realize that there's only one half inch of glass separating you from this impressive beast. Because there are so many gorillas in the exhibit, the odds of one wanting to lean in close are very good. On those rare occasions when I have the time to visit the Bronx Zoo, I'll spend half an hour or more just standing there, waiting for a gorilla to become curious about me.

Another species that has helped zoos attract more visitors is the panda. Several zoos across the country have pandas, but there is a big difference with this species compared to others. Those zoos don't own the pandas. A zoo can only lease a pair of pandas from the Chinese government, and the cost is a whopping one million dollars per year. In order to justify spending that kind of money, the zoo with pandas has to go to extraordinary measures to make sure the exhibit is going to attract big crowds. Visitors are usually charged an extra fee to see the pandas, and, of course, there are concession stands selling anything and everything related to pandas—including panda ice cream. If the pandas have a baby, that baby has to go back to China when it's mature enough to travel. The baby pandas grow up to produce more pandas, and then new adults are available to be leased to the United States. In essence, the American zoo is a surrogate mother.

Visitors to the panda exhibit might like to think that such exhibits are helping this endangered species to survive in the wild. This could not be further from the truth. A panda born in captivity has no chance of survival in the wild. It's only chance to come off the endangered species list is to produce so many pandas in captivity that the species continues on, but pandas in the wild could still disappear without preserving their habitat.

Protecting and preserving unusual and endangered species is what often inspires those with financial means to create their own private zoos. The late John Aspinall in England created Howletts Zoo so that he could literally interact with the animals he collected. He would go into the enclosure with gorillas and play with them. He did the same thing with tigers, although one of his zookeepers was killed when trying to feed or care for those tigers. But no one could prevent John from doing what he wanted, because he owned the zoo. He also bred elephants and rhinoceroses and created comfortable habitats for them and all his animals. If people wanted to visit his zoo, that was fine, but he didn't need their patronage to survive.

My friend John the art dealer with the lynx also had a private zoo in Africa. He collected from all over the world those animals he wanted to observe and visit. One of his favorite animals was his male African elephant, Boobers, for whom he built a five-acre enclosure. If Boobers wanted to knock down trees, he could. His mate, Jackie, was in the enclosure with him; so if Boobers wanted to mate, he could do so whenever he felt like it. The owner didn't have to satisfy any visitors, so his animals lived optimal lives on their terms.

Another private zoo owner in Malaysia wanted to breed servals, so I provided him with a breeding pair. Another owner in Japan wanted to acquire Gila monsters and Mexican beaded lizards, and I provided him with those species. I have exported any number of species to private zoos around the world. For obvious reasons, I really can't reveal who the owners are or exactly where their zoos are located. Private zoos have always offered an alternative way of collecting and displaying animals.

As zoos look to the future, one important consideration is for them to use their revenues to help animals in the wild. This is what Gerald Durrell did. He would go to more remote areas like Mauritius or Round Island in the Seychelles, where there were odd and rare animals like the pink pigeon or the Round Island skink. From his zoo earnings, the sales of his books, and private donations he had solicited, he would then give sufficient monies to the governments to protect the habitats of these animals. At the same time, he built up his breeding populations just in case these animals went extinct in the wild, thus ensuring a stable population in captivity. Today, it could be said that corrupt governments might appropriate those monies and the animals would not be protected after all. The simple answer is ecotourism. People from all over the world are willing to travel to exotic locations in order to see endangered species "in the wild." Everyone wants and needs to make a sustainable living, including the natives in some remote area where there is a species to be preserved. Burning down a habitat to make palm oil can be traded for maintaining an animal habitat if there's money in it. Zoos can become the saviors of dwindling species.

Another big change for zoos is the way habitats are created. For Durrell, his zoo in the Channel Islands displayed mostly smaller animals that could be kept in roomy cages and could easily be viewed by the public. Americans tend to prefer observing bigger animals, and this preference has over the past several years attracted animal rights groups who objected to the unnatural confinement of these large species. Not wanting to lose their audience, and their very existence, zoos began creating habitats more in concert with the animal's wild environments. Presumably, the animals are much happier, but new problems have been created.

Most recently, and with much fanfare, the Central Park Zoo in New York City acquired three snow leopards that are housed in a habitat that authentically replicates their natural home in areas of Kashmir and Nepal. There are three spacious viewing areas that afford three different views, behind glass, into the snow leopards' abode. By all standards, the habitat is beautifully and faithfully re-created—with one significant problem.

As Peter Matthiessen so well documented in his best-selling memoir *The Snow Leopard,* this creature is legendary for its solitary and elusive existence. Along with naturalist George Schaller and others who have followed in their footsteps, these two men spent the better part of two years trying to view one of these magnificent animals. Even today, there is scant camera footage of snow leopards in the wild. They are masters of camouflage and are reclusive beyond the extremes of Howard Hughes. When the snow leopard exhibit opened in June 2009, the crowds were understandably large and enthusiastic. My coauthor, Nancy Ellis-Bell, was there; and along with all the other hopefuls, she was disappointed that there was no sighting. Still, she understood from her longtime fascination with these animals that such a sighting was unlikely. I doubt the rest of the disappointed viewers were as understanding. Most Americans are not willing to sit for hours in hopes of seeing the tip of a tail against some foliage. They want to see the animal and they want to see it now. When I was a child at the Bronx Zoo, I saw all of the animals, up close and personal. It may not have been so good for the animals; but like the rest of the people there, I left with a smile on my face.

An increasing number of zoos display their animals in that way, posting a sign indicating what is inside the habitat. Like those eager characters in *Jurassic Park,* the question becomes, "I presume we will see dinosaurs at some point." In most modern zoos, the animals are too far away or are hidden from view by natural vegetation. Animal rights people are applauding. Everyday Americans are walking away unsatisfied. Progressive zoos are thus becoming living museums, not unlike New York City's American Museum of Natural History, where animals are featured in dioramas.

Breeding zoo animals has become almost nonexistent because there's no place to put them. Animals bred in captivity can't be put back into the wild. The California condor is a perfect case in point. This bird was driven to the point of extinction primarily because there was no place left for it to live. Having evolved in the southwest part of the United States, condors lived off large, dead mammals that were plentiful a hundred years ago. In more recent years, many of them were also shot by humans, along with the bison and pronghorn antelopes on which the condors fed. Breeding grounds also disappeared in the face of real estate development. Ultimately, there were twelve condors left and extinction was imminent.

These remaining condors were sent to the wild animal park at the San Diego Zoo, where they bred prolifically, resulting in lots of these stork-like birds. Now the problem wasn't extinction; it was overpopulation.

"We'll turn them loose. After all, they're wild creatures."

At face value, that solution may have looked reasonable, but an important fact had been overlooked. Some animals are able to adapt to changing situations. Those who are more specialized, like the condors, cannot. The condors are not able to adapt to a new, wild world. Wild foods and nesting sites for wild condors are scarce. Their only salvation from extinction is to remain in zoos or in the little bit of wild that is left but still managed by humans.

One possibility is for the zoos to modify their natural habitats to feature enticements: a heated rock to lure the big cat out of the bushes, random feeding times so that the animal comes out of hiding more frequently, and food placement in different locations so the animal has to "hunt." The random feeding routine is working well for wolves, and thus is keeping the customers happy.

The other possibility is to adopt the philosophy of circuses, where entertainment becomes the focus, and customers feel that they have been both informed and amused.* SeaWorld is an excellent example of zoo-meets-circus. All day long there are shows featuring animals, and information is offered by those conducting the shows. At SeaWorld the customer can feed a stingray, get up close and personal with otters and sea lions, and walk away feeling as if he or she has been "in the wild." Going back for a moment to the snow leopard exhibit, perhaps the zoo should consider installing a little chamber, out of which pops a chicken neck during prime viewing times. Zoos won't survive with a little rustling in the bushes. We have to see the dinosaurs.

Given the tug between displaying the animal and experiencing the animal, the circus approach seems to be a viable choice for survival. Just recently, the Franklin Park Zoo in Boston—a very old and venerable institution—announced it might have to close.

---

*True, there are those who assert that such shows abuse or stress their animals. Admittedly, such assertions are correct in a small number of cases; but in my experience, circus owners are most protective of the animals in their care, as their livelihoods depend on these animals.

As more zoos close, more animals are displaced, and the remedy for that displacement is not pretty.

Even in my pet store, Sundays have become a kind of "circus day." Every Sunday, I make myself and my animals available for holding and petting. Maybe not the dangerous or biting ones, but many of my animals can be touched and observed up close. I become the ringmaster, sharing with the child or adult as much of my knowledge as I can. Even though my sales that day are typically low, I feel that it's more important to let people experience the animals and learn more about them. Zoos need to reassess the American public, and cater to their desires. Gerald Durrell was able to maintain his zoo because he understood the people who could keep him in business. Modern zoos would do well to follow his lead.

CHAPTER 39

Circus Secrets and
the Saga of Siegfried and Roy

While zoos continue to hold a negative connotation for many people, circuses have it even worse. Whether it's Ringling Brothers and Barnum & Bailey or some other circus, even those who love to go to circuses seem to feel guilty about how the animals are handled in order to make them perform. Those same people also worry about how the animals are housed, and how they're treated in general. I've had considerable firsthand experience with circus owners and trainers, and here's what I know.

I think it is unfair to disparage the people who entertain us with performing animals. Exceptions should not dictate the rule. Consider the bears in the Moscow Circus.

I remember attending a performance by a Russian circus troupe that featured dancing bears. One bear in particular, named Gosha, was a full-grown adult male Russian brown bear. He wore a muzzle, as did all the Russian bears, and I had to laugh. In no way would the muzzle prevent the bear from killing the trainer; his claws were six inches long. He was also very tall and stood at least a foot taller than the trainer. What impressed me was that the bear was having the time of his life. The bear and the trainer were hugging and kissing each other, and there was no way to produce that interaction with any kind of cruel training. The best trick was the bear lying on its back and the trainer putting a wand with fire at both ends on the bear's back paws. The bear spun that wand for the longest time, and I still don't know how someone could train a bear to do something like that. Then the bear would stand up, without being goaded, and perform cute little dances. I went backstage later to meet Gosha and his trainer, and the chemistry and love between them was exactly the same as it had been on stage. I can't speak for all bear performers, but Gosha looked like he was smiling.

Another circus animal that people think is mistreated is the elephant. Without a doubt, the circus elephant is the most valuable animal in the circus. A performing elephant can't be taken out of the wild and then trained. Those elephants must be born in captivity, often to the circus itself. Ringling Brothers and Barnam & Bailey, for example, breeds its own elephants. A female Asian elephant is easily worth hundreds of thousands of dollars and represents the biggest animal draw for the circus owner. If something happens to that elephant that prevents it from performing, or if it should die, the owner can't go out and acquire a new one. Consequently, that owner isn't going to jeopardize his income by injuring one of those elephants. Again, I'm not saying that cruelty doesn't occur, but certainly it is not as commonplace as many people choose to believe, and since I personally have never trained or worked with elephants, I cannot judge people who do.

Circus animals are like city dogs in Manhattan. These dogs mostly live in tiny apartments, and they are always on a leash when they're outside. Even my dogs, which have a backyard, don't see anything except the eight-foot fence outside and the inside of my house. Most of the dogs I'm familiar with live much less interesting lives than circus animals do.

Circus animals are always traveling from one place to another, seeing new things and interacting with other animals in creative ways. Sure, when they're actually traveling, their cages are small; but most of that time they're sleeping anyway.

Let's go back to the city dog for a minute. In the morning before he or she goes to work, the owner puts a leash on the dog and takes it for a walk. So, here's this dog on the streets of New York City where he's constantly smelling, learning, smelling, learning. The streets are like his canine Internet. Then it's back to the apartment, where he sleeps until a dog walker comes later in the day. Now he's back on a leash, but this time there are four or five other dogs joining him. And now they're all smelling and learning, smelling and learning, and sharing information with one another.

"Did you smell this?"

"Did you smell that?"

I can just imagine their doggie conversations. After their group walk they're back to the apartment for another nap, waiting patiently for their owner to return home at the end of the day. Then comes another walk, and more canine Internet surfing. Bedtime arrives, and the cycle starts over again the next day.

My dogs, like many suburban dogs, see the same walls, the same furniture, the same bushes, the same fence every day. They probably don't even get to see other dogs. They might as well live on a dogless Pluto.

Back to circuses, I believe what I see with my own eyes. Most people who make allegations of cruelty against circus owners or trainers believe propaganda from other people who don't believe that animals should ever be commodities. That's a big issue. Too many Americans, in particular, see animals as quasi-humans. That's just not valid. For thousands of years, across every culture imaginable, animals have been viewed as commodities. We as humans have evolved to where we are today because we embraced animals as commodities, not as "human" partners. I'm not saying that cruelty doesn't occur in circuses; I'm sure it does. I'm only suggesting that those with special-interest causes may have exaggerated the instances of cruelty.

With the circuses I've been to, I've spent time with the people who train animals, and their knowledge of the animals they work with is vast. Many of them know more about those animals than some zoologists and scientists do. They understand the reality of working with a five-hundred-pound tiger.

Like Siegfried and Roy in Las Vegas. I don't think anyone knows more about big cats than they do. Their cats are incredibly well trained, but they're not domesticated. Even the cubs born into their household are not domesticated. People forget that. Just because an animal is born into captivity doesn't make it domesticated. They're still wild, and they need to be watched carefully.

This whole circus issue comes down to whether or not humans should coerce animals into performing. Whether the animal is dancing on its back legs or just standing there looking at people— like in a zoo—it's still performing. For the animal in question, it's all the same. Circuses are there to entertain us, not teach us lessons about animals and life. There's nothing wrong with being entertained.

CHAPTER 40

The Pantheon of Animal "Deities"

So many great names in animal behavior have shaped me. My personal pantheon of animal greats starts, of course, with Gerald Durrell. After I read his book, while I was still in high school, I knew that I had found a kindred spirit. From the time he was a child, he was fascinated with animals, collecting and observing them. It's reported that his first word was *zoo*. Whether or not it was truly his first word, we certainly know that a zoo was his dream from an early age. As an adult, he went on collecting expeditions, financed by a small inheritance, in order to acquire animals he could sell to zoos. At the beginning, his mission was not conservation and breeding endangered species in captivity; he was learning all that he could about the animals he collected. Later, when he saw that the zoos to which he was selling were merely warehousing the animals until they died, he determined to find a way to have his own zoo, one where the animals would have a good life and where he could learn more about them. So he wrote books and persuaded people to donate money, and his zoo was no longer an impossible dream. Had he not gone to West Africa to collect animals for zoos in order to make money, he wouldn't have had the money to write the books that made him even more money, and that ultimately led him to establish his own zoo.

First, he built a gorilla breeding habitat, then a lemur habitat, and then a habitat for marmosets. Then he took a trip to the Seychelles, in the Indian Ocean, to acquire endangered skinks and snakes that he could breed in captivity. Eventually, his zoo on the island of Jersey in the Channel Islands became not only a breeding habitat for numerous species, but also a source of knowledge and entertainment for the public. Although the zoo is still there, it's not the same. After Durrell died, the zoo became a pale version of the stellar environment it was when he was alive.

Another animal lover with his own zoo is my longtime friend Bernie Levine. A vet by profession, he owned a pet farm back in the 1970s and '80s. In reality, it was a series of quarantine stations where he kept the thousands and thousands of birds and other animals that he had imported from other countries. After the quarantine period was over, he would sell them to zoos and pet stores all over the United States. He eventually stopped that business and bought a small zoo of sorts in Miami. It was called Parrot Jungle, and it had only birds when he acquired it. Parrot Jungle soon became Jungle Island, and his new zoo displayed tigers, orangutans, chimpanzees, birds of every kind, and a whole host of exotic animals. The one animal he's never been able to obtain, and which he sorely wanted, was a gorilla, one of the only concessions he's had to make to his dream.

One of my other major influences was the famous Austrian ethnologist Konrad Lorenz. His book *King Solomon's Ring* was one of my greatest inspirations when I was a child. According to ancient lore, King Solomon had a special ring that allowed him to understand the languages of animals. Lorenz himself made all kinds of amazing discoveries about animals, mostly about birds. Like Durrell, he was an astute observer of nature, and he could be mesmerized by something as simple as the hamsters that lived in a vivarium on his desk. He would sit there literally for hours, watching the golden hamster and her ten babies eating, playing, licking one another, and just being content. In another corner of his office was a small aviary that housed a pair of long-tailed titmice sitting on their nest with three eggs in it. He had bred them in captivity, as he did other animals. From him and Alba Ballard, I learned everything I could ever want to know about birds.

Alba Ballard was a force unto herself. She came to the United States from Milan, where her father owned a zoo. From a very young age, she was comfortable with species from wolves to Andean condors. Birds were her great love, and that is how she and I came to meet, here in the United States. Although I didn't meet her until my teens, she had been living around the corner from me since I'd been a child. She possessed a truly magical gift for understanding birds and had well over fifty of them. Some lived comfortably in her expansive downstairs, others became performing birds she dressed up in little costumes, and at least one other, Joker, she begged from me. Every time one of my birds extends and beats its wings, I think of Alba dubbing the motion "flap-flap." Alba was not only an animal mentor, she was a dear friend.

Another dear friend, fortunately still alive, is the well-known host and animal expert Jim Fowler. When I was just a little kid, I would watch him on cable television, never dreaming that I would someday become his friend. On Sundays, after Grandpa and I had gone fishing, we'd go back home and first watch *Lassie,* then Mutual of Omaha's *Wild Kingdom*. Along with Marlin Perkins, Jim would enthrall me with his knowledge and animal adventures. Thirty years later, after seeing me on my own cable television show, he contacted me. I was flabbergasted. I didn't realize that he lived in Connecticut, and now he was interested in appearing on my cable television show, where he continued teaching me things about animals. Probably the most important thing he taught me was how to present myself to the public. He has a gift for that, knowing how to present information and himself in the best way. I am so grateful for that, and to have him as a friend.

Another dear friend and animal great, sadly now deceased, was Roger Caras. During the time I knew him he was president of the ASPCA in Manhattan. He had also written sixty books, and he was without doubt the most well-educated man on the subject of animals, whether wild animals or pets. I loved listening to him speak. Each and every word came out carefully polished and perfect. Few people can hold me in thrall; he could.

I originally met him through a mutual acquaintance, Marie Killilea, who wrote a best-selling book called *Karen*, published in the early 1950s, about her daughter with cerebral palsy. This was twenty-five years ago, and she had called me asking to buy an African Grey for her daughter on the recommendation of a veterinarian who knew me well. When it came to erudition, Marie and her husband, Jimmy, were a lot like Roger Caras; in fact, they were friends. I loved being around the Killileas, being able to share my knowledge with them and learn from them. On one of those occasions, Roger joined us, and I felt so honored to meet this giant of a man. Apparently, he was equally impressed with me, and he later asked to appear on my television show, *Metro Pets*. In contrast to his network television appearances, he loved being on my show because he could be himself. He didn't have to flatter or cajole, as was so often required in the big leagues.

I especially remember one segment where he and I were sitting with my menagerie of the day, and talking about people who keep pit bulls and teach them to be mean. Suddenly, Roger exclaimed, and I quote:

"If you have a large dog that can do damage, and you teach that dog to be nasty, to be aggressive, then you are a moron. And on your mailbox in front of your house, it should say, 'Mr. and Mrs. Moron.' "

That segment can still be seen on YouTube under the title "Marc Morrone's guest says funny things."

Roger is also well remembered by the people at the Westminster Kennel Club Dog Show for his creative script about terriers. Since all terriers are very much the same, all bred for the same purpose, and all from the same area, Roger had to be creative to make the script interesting and informative. The last time I went to Westminster to do some tapings for Martha, all I kept thinking was how empty the place seemed without Roger's booming voice coming over the loudspeaker.

Martha certainly doesn't have a booming voice, but she most certainly has a booming personality, albeit expressed in quiet tones. I'm sure most people think that Martha's fascination with animals is some kind of aberration. I've never discussed that with her, but I know from firsthand experience that she shares with me that special animal gene. When I watch her handle animals, it's clear. She'll just grab an animal without any thought of, "Does it bite?" She's comfortable in her own skin and with theirs. She also "grabbed" me and taught me how to present myself in front of a camera, giving me a forum in which I can share knowledge. In only six minutes, I can demonstrate how to brush a cat's teeth or how to check for signs of potential health issues in nine different animals, with Harry on one shoulder and two Siamese kittens on the other. Martha, along with producers Barbara Fight and Jocelyn Santos, has given me to the world in a much bigger way than I could have ever done on my own.

The last of my animal heroes, also sadly deceased, is Steve Irwin, the Crocodile Hunter. In the beginning, he had to do something to get people's attention, so he went in search of crocodiles he could wrestle, poisonous snakes he could wrangle, whatever made him money so he could pursue his dream of having his own zoo. From wrestling and wrangling, he moved into sharing knowledge and teaching people about wild animals. Crocodiles and snakes aside, he could take the smallest, most mundane animal and make it seem fascinating to the public. Ironically, Jim Fowler has said the same thing about me.

"That Marc Morrone, he can take a rabbit and make it seem interesting."

In pursuit of his ultimate zoo, Irwin started out with a little reptile park. As his reputation increased, so did the size and diversity of his zoo. Now he had tigers and elephants, and other impressive animals. He didn't have to get board approval for anything. If he wanted to acquire a particular animal to study and learn about, he bought it. The only animals he chose not to acquire were birds. You could see that he wasn't comfortable around them, and the feeling was mutual.

As his zoo expanded, he needed to make more and more money to support it; and toward the end of his life, things were a lot more complicated than they had been in the beginning. It seemed as if he was doing shows he didn't especially want to do, and he was becoming so busy with the business side of life that he wasn't getting enough time to enjoy his animals and his family.

I still remember a Larry King segment that took place while Steve's daughter, Bindi, was very young. Steve had said how much his daughter loved growing up at the zoo, and how much she loved all the animals.

"She's growing up like Mowgli."

Larry King looked at him blankly and asked, "Who's Mowgli?"

Obviously, he never read Rudyard Kipling's *The Jungle Book,* as Steve had.

In many ways, people didn't understand Steve Irwin. When he was tragically killed while swimming above a stingray, there were murmurings of "arrogant" and "careless." Nothing could be further from the truth. He was doing exactly what he loved to do. He died celebrating the life he had chosen. It was simply a random event, something he completely understood.

Before his death, I tried to connect with him, and later with Bindi, when they were in New York, but it never quite worked out. I imagined the three of us doing a special on Australian animals, with bearded dragons, carpet pythons, cockatiels, parakeets, rose-breasted cockatoos, kookaburras, and sugar gliders. It would have been great fun.

Bindi is very much like her father, like me, and like others with that obsessive animal gene. Maybe she and I can do that segment someday.

In the meantime, I am proud to carry on the good work of all of my mentors—as teacher, as media personality, and as the pet keeper.

CHAPTER 41

Vision of a Pet Keeper

One of the problems with movies about or starring animals is that they help to exacerbate existing misconceptions about animal behavior. *Lady and the Tramp* has dogs engaged in conversations that are very un-dog-like. Even if dogs could talk, they wouldn't have cognitive discussions. For all animals it's a matter of instinct, not intellect.

The other day I watched a squirrel burying nuts for the winter. Wrong! I watched a squirrel burying nuts. Period. The squirrel has no concept of "saving for a rainy day." That's a human concept that many people superimpose on the squirrel's instinctive behavior. Years and years of genetic modification have selected out the squirrels that have learned to survive by being able to retrieve their buried nuts. The only reason he's hiding them is that he can't eat them all at once, and he's protecting them from other animals. Come winter, he'll start digging in the ground to find new food—and, surprise! There will be the nuts he buried in May. He doesn't have a memory track that tells him where he buried the nuts in the first place. He's simply buried so many that the odds of finding some are on his side.

When people say to me, "My dog spitefully pooped on the rug," or "My bird is spitefully screaming at me," I always offer the same response: "Your dog had to go to the bathroom and didn't see any other option. Your bird has learned that when it makes noise, it gets attention. Whether you pet him or scream back at him, it's all attention to him." It's all about cause and effect without the benefit of cognition. If we can just view the world through the animal's eyes—not his brain—we will live with animals more amicably, and with much less stress.

Animals are also "in the moment." If you punish your dog for pooping in the morning, by afternoon he's completely forgotten about it. He's not "angry" with you, and he's not going to plot his revenge. The dog will become totally house-trained either out of routine or out of positive reinforcement. Whichever it is, the new, improved behavior was born out of some instinct, such as self-protection or the need for food.

Parrots, which are much smarter than dogs, figure things out faster. But it's still about their preservation in your habitat.

The problem with television programs like *The Dog Whisperer* with Cesar Millan, and Victoria Stilwell's show on Animal Planet, is that they give the viewer the impression that the offending dog has been cured of barking or some other undesirable habit in one hour. In truth, Victoria spent at least a week filming that "cure," and Cesar's remedy for bad behavior takes much longer than the show indicates. Most Americans want Band-Aid solutions in cyber-fast time.

My favorite dog-barking cure is to keep a squirt bottle of water at hand. Say "no!" and squirt. It's surefire. And it is fast.

So, if animals function primarily out of instinct, training and behavior modification aside, then we quickly come up against a theological assertion: God created humans in His image, and He created animals for humans to use. Animal husbandry and pet keeping both assert that we must use animals in a humane manner. They're not beneath us; they're just different. There is no justification for being cruel to any living creature. Good pet keepers understand that we must "protect" the animals who "serve" us, realizing that their instincts are to live safely and well.

Every creature on the planet uses some other creature. That's nature. Breeders and pet stores sell animals to people. That's commerce. Commerce is good; but for some people, designating animals as commodities is an affront.

What's most important here is realizing that the more we understand animals, the more we understand ourselves, and by extension our world and our humanity.

For the most part, humans want too many answers. It goes back to "Why do bad things happen to good people?" and "Why do good things happen to bad people?" By tossing ourselves back and forth on the horns of this dilemma, we just end up making ourselves miserable. I continue to be impressed by people caught up in tragedy who simply move on. No complaining, no blame, and no desire for revenge. Here in New York, for example, I have become friends with many Jews who are Holocaust survivors. What always amazes me is how they describe that experience, if they do at all. Mostly, it's a matter of "It happened, it was terrible, and we survived. Here we are." I think that is the healthiest attitude for life. Like me, they just wanted their lives to be useful, to be meaningful. And I see a parallel in the animal world: animals just want to be.

When those geese literally brought down that airplane over the Hudson River early in 2009, many of the geese in that migrating flock continued on their way to a warmer climate. They didn't pull over in the next clearing to lament the fate of the other geese or celebrate their own good luck. When feathers sent to the Smithsonian were tested, it was determined that the geese in question were indeed migrating from the North Pole. Now the people who wanted to kill the resident geese in the area changed their minds.

"It's okay. The problem was 'migrating' geese."

It could just as easily have been a group of resident geese. The real problem is that the airports have been built around marshy areas that house geese. The geese who died were caught up in a random event.

That's the last significant point to remember about animal behavior. All animals accept random behavior. No whimper, no squawk. The dog didn't get his treat today. Dog doesn't sulk; he lies down somewhere and licks himself. Parrot didn't get his peanuts today. Parrot eats something else in the dish. That look he's giving you isn't disappointment or pique. He's just looking up before he dives back into the food dish.

Finding Nemo is a perfect example of how animals "think." When Marlin says about his missing son, "I promised him I would never let anything bad happen to him," Dory responds with, "Well, how could you promise something like that? If something bad didn't happen, then nothing would ever happen."

Out of the mouths of fish.

It's important for people to understand what Marlin was saying, and how that relates to us as pet keepers. One of the reasons we like pets so much is because owning a pet is one of the few things in our lives that is not random. Having a dog or a cat or a bird at home, or a tank full of fish, becomes one consistent aspect of your life. When you come home from work, the dog will wag its tail, the cat will rub up against you, the bird will say "hello," and the fish will rush up to the glass to be fed. Every day, you'll receive that kind of acknowledgment and gratitude. Your day away from home may have included a flat tire, a surprise visit from some kind of inspector, or a run-in with your boss, but when you get back home, the world is predictable and accepting. Whatever control is lacking in your workday is always there at home.

That control and consistency require a third "c" word: complement. A good pet must complement our lives, not complicate them. A good pet must make our lives better, never worse. Otherwise, the random chaos of our workday will simply continue on when we get home. If your friends won't come over to visit, or if they visit but "grimace" at the sight of chewed furniture, or if they're constantly pushing down a jumping dog, it's time to reevaluate your method of "pet keeping."

The truth is many people turn a blind eye to their pets' behavior. I make it a point not to do that. My house is literally perfect. Martha Stewart's house is literally perfect. We both have beautiful furniture that is untouched by beaks or teeth or claws. We have curtains that go from ceiling to floor, and are in pristine condition. We have lovely upholstered chairs, and every thread is in place. And Martha and I have a houseful of animals. How do we do it?

Our cats are not declawed, which is nothing more than compensating for bad behavior. We have cat trees that have been inoculated with catnip for the cats to climb on. We also have "scat mats" with tiny nine-volt batteries that discourage cats from jumping up where they shouldn't. Most cats want to be on the tallest object around. The cat tree gives them both a scratching and a perching place. Our birds stay in their cages unless we are there to supervise them. Our dogs either stay behind barriers or in their crates when they're not interacting with us. My only exception to all of the above is the kitchen table, where I do allow my cats to visit with me when I'm in the kitchen. Martha does the same thing. Not when we have guests, of course. It's just our little peccadillo.

Another aspect to prime pet keeping is equality. I treat all of my animals equally. I don't think that a parakeet is somehow less deserving of respect than a big parrot. I don't think that a mouse is less deserving than a dog. I can appreciate a tank full of exotic fish, and I can appreciate a tank full of guppies. All animals deserve equal care and equal fascination, because they're all fascinating animals in their own right. If I were to lose everything I have and had to move into a tiny trailer, I would still have a five-gallon tank of guppies or a parakeet or a pigeon or a hamster and be content as a pet keeper.

God created us all, and I don't discriminate.

AFTERWORD

When I started my animal odyssey at age four, all I wanted to do was to learn everything I could about every possible kind of animal. Today, at age fifty, I have indeed learned everything I possibly could up to this point. Everything I've wanted to do so far, I've done. There may not be a zoo in my future, but there will always be animals in my life.

Whether it's fish or ferrets, the reality of pet keeping is that the passion must ultimately be the reward. The onslaught of big pet store chains and the influence of the Internet has made the world of independent pet stores as precarious as that of independent bookstores. Throngs of people come into my store every day, asking for information and learning about the animals I have in my store. Some of them buy an animal from me or purchase supplies for their pets. Either way, I am happy to spend time with them, not really that focused on making a sale, but on helping them to become better pet keepers. That's what Alba Ballard told me I had to do. That was her loving "curse." Ultimately, what's in it for me as a pet keeper is to improve the relationship between animals and people.

I am blessed that my wife shares this passion and that my son at least likes animals. He has been spared the aberrant gene that dominates my life. His future is probably a little more secure than mine.

My life will always be about pet keeping. Even if I lost everything, I would still have my family. Our new life might be simpler, and might include fewer animals, but my vision and mission would be intact. If all I could have as pets were a few guppies in a tank, I would appreciate and enjoy those. If I couldn't own a pet store, I would still share my knowledge with anyone who asked. Beyond anyone asking, I would continue to reach out to the world with what I've learned about animals. That is my calling.

I like to believe that I'm keeping alive the legacies of Gerald Durrell, Alba Ballard, Wendy Winstead, the Crocodile Hunter, my great-great grandfather, my grandfather, and others who have formed me. I am grateful to all of those people who love and support me, whether or not I've ever met them in person. I am also grateful to my media family—Martha Stewart, Jocelyn Santos, Barbara Fight, and all of those who have given me to the world in a bigger way than I ever could have done on my own.

I am not just the pet keeper; I am the man for all species, in whatever form that takes. I am content.

ACKNOWLEDGMENTS

First, to Martha Stewart for her immeasurable influence in helping me become who I am today. Second, to my literary agent and coauthor, Nancy Ellis-Bell, for her bulldog determination to see this project come to life. Third, to Alba Ballard for her wisdom and friendship. Fourth, to Roger Caras for his inspiration and broad knowledge of so many species. Fifth, to Evan Hennessey and Kathy Rothstein of Sten-Tel Transcription Service, without whom this book could not have been written so well. Sixth, to the U.S. Fish and Wildlife Service, the United States Department of Agriculture, and the New York State Department of Environmental Conservation for granting me the permits to allow me to conduct the activities that help make me the person I am today. Seventh, to Jocelyn Santos and Barbara Fight, who created a TV personalty out of somebody who was not really very special at all.

Finally, to all of my family and friends—you all know who you are—for all of your love and support throughout the years.

ABOUT THE AUTHORS

MARC MORRONE currently owns Parrots of the World, a pet store in Rockville Centre, New York, that he boasts is the cleanest in the universe. His whole life has been lived in the pursuit of learning about all sorts of animals, using his pet store as his laboratory. His passion was discovered by Martha Stewart, who has featured him regularly on her TV and radio shows and in her magazines, where he does the best he can to share his knowledge about pets and the natural world using the different media available to him.

Visit him at www.ParrotsoftheWorld.com and www.MarcMorrone.com.

NANCY ELLIS-BELL is the author of *The Parrot Who Thought She Was a Dog* (Harmony Books) and a respected literary agent. She lives in northern California with her menagerie of animals and a very understanding husband. Nancy convinced Marc Morrone that his story would make a fascinating book. Then Marc convinced her to help him write it.

Visit her at www.TheBarkingParrot.com.